WELCOME

Congratulations on starting your journey to become an AWS Certified Solutions Architect. You now have access to the essential exam training for the **AWS Certified Solutions Architect Associate (SAA-C03)**.

This popular training resource includes the Exam Cram (this document) and, as a bonus, access to the video course online from Digital Cloud Training. Together, these powerful learning tools will maximize your chances of passing your exam on your first attempt.

You will learn everything you need to know, both in theory and practice, to succeed in the exam. The video course includes **24 hours of theory lessons**, guided hands-on labs, and quiz questions to test your knowledge.

With a strong, hands-on focus, you'll learn how to architect and build applications on Amazon Web Services, fully preparing you for the AWS exam. By the end of the course, you will have developed strong AWS skills and the confidence to pass your AWS Certified Solutions Architect Associate exam.

More than 1,000,000 students have trusted our resources to achieve their AWS certifications. Through diligent study of these learning materials, you will be in the perfect position to ace your exam.

Wishing you all the best on your cloud journey!

Neal Davis

Neal Davis

Founder of Digital Cloud Training

Limited Time Bonus Offer - FREE Access to Video Course

To help you best prepare for your AWS Certified Solutions Architect Associate certification exam, we're offering free access to our popular video course, which includes 24 hours of instructor-led lessons, to all students who purchase this book.

Navigate to the BONUS OFFER at the end of this book for instructions on how to access the video course.

What do other Students say?

Check out the excellent reviews from our many students who passed their AWS exams:

☆☆☆☆☆

The course is all-embracing and covers all there's to know and equip a Solution Architect for the exam and in-work experience. Neal Davis is a thorough teacher and applies working teaching strategies to drive home the salient and needed points for the exam.

☆☆☆☆☆

I've just passed my CSAA exam using this course and the practice exam course. This course is an absolute must for anyone sitting this exam. The depth of the coverage is really impressive, and the time taken to prepare it and attention to detail are phenomenal. I can't recommend this enough.

☆☆☆☆☆

The course content is of high standard and I very much like the diagrams, explanations, and the practical lab sessions. The practical approach fits my learning style and makes it far easier to retain the knowledge needed for the exam.

☆☆☆☆☆

Very detailed training, very well-formatted training videos and practice exercises with clear instructions. So far, the number 1 course.

☆☆☆☆☆

Just passed the AWS Certified Solutions Architect Associate. This course is amazing. The knowledge is to the point and deep.

TABLE OF CONTENTS

Welcome 1
   Limited Time Bonus Offer - FREE Access to Video Course 2
   What do other Students say? 2

Table of Contents 3

Getting Started 11
   Your Pathway to Success 11
   Contact, Support & Feedback 13
   Reviews Really Matter 13
   Connect with the AWS Community 13

The SAA-C03 Exam Version 15
   Test Domains and Objectives 16

About Exam Crams 18

AWS Identity and Access Management (IAM) 19
   AWS Identity and Access Management (AWS IAM) 19
   AWS IAM Best Practices 21

Amazon Elastic Compute Cloud (EC2) 22
   Amazon EC2 22
   Benefits of Amazon EC2 22
   Public, Private and Elastic IP addresses 23
   EC2 Placement Groups 23
   NAT Instance vs NAT Gateway 24
   EC2 Instance Lifecycle 24
   AWS Nitro System 26
   AWS Nitro Enclaves 26
   Amazon EC2 Pricing Options 27
   Dedicated Instances and Dedicated Hosts 27

Elastic Load Balancing, and Auto Scaling 29

Amazon EC2 Auto Scaling 29

Auto Scaling - Monitoring 29

Additional Scaling Settings 30

Elastic Load Balancing 30

ELB Use Cases 31

Cross-Zone Load Balancing 32

AWS Organizations 33

Consolidated Billing 33

Service Control Policies 33

AWS Organizations - Migration 34

Amazon Virtual Private Cloud (VPC) 35

Amazon VPC 35

Amazon VPC Components 35

Rules and Guidelines (IP CIDR) 36

Additional Considerations 36

Security Groups vs Network ACLs 36

VPC Connectivity – AWS Managed VPN 37

VPC Connectivity – AWS Direct Connect 37

VPC Connectivity – DX + VPN 38

VPC Connectivity – VPN CloudHub 38

VPC Connectivity – Software VPN 38

VPC Connectivity – Transit VPC 39

VPC Connectivity – VPC Peering 39

VPC Connectivity – VPC Endpoints 40

VPC Flow Logs 40

Amazon Simple Storage Service (S3) 41

S3 Buckets 41

S3 Objects 41

S3 Storage Classes 42

IAM / Bucket Policies 42

S3 Access Control Lists (ACLs) 43

When to use each access control mechanism 43

S3 Versioning 43

S3 Lifecycle Management 44

S3 LM: Supported Transitions 44

S3 LM: Unsupported Transitions 44

S3 Multi-Factor Authentication Delete (MFA Delete) 45

S3 Multi-Factor Authentication Delete (MFA Delete) 46

MFA-Protected API Access 46

S3 Encryption 46

S3 Default Encryption 47

S3 Event Notifications 47

S3 Multipart Upload 48

S3 Transfer Acceleration 48

S3 Copy API 49

Server Access Logging 49

CORS with Amazon S3 49

Cross Account Access Methods 49

S3 Performance Optimizations 50

DNS, Caching, and Performance Optimization 51

Amazon Route 53 51

Route 53 Hosted Zones 51

Route 53 Health Checks 51

CNAME vs Alias Records 52

Amazon Route 53 Routing Policies 52

Amazon CloudFront Caching 53

Caching Based on Request Headers 53

CloudFront Signed URLs / Cookies 53

Lambda@Edge 54

Block and File Storage 55

Amazon EBS 55

Amazon EBS SSD-Backed Volumes 55

Amazon EBS HDD-Backed Volumes 55

Amazon Data Lifecycle Manager (DLM) 56

EBS vs instance store 56

Amazon Machine Images (AMIs) 57

EBS Snapshots 57

Using RAID with EBS 57

EBS Encryption 58

Amazon Elastic File System (EFS) 58

EFS Access Control 59

EFS Encryption 59

AWS DataSync 59

Amazon FSx 59

Amazon FSx for Windows File Server 60

Amazon FSx for Lustre 60

AWS Storage Gateway – File Gateway 60

AWS Storage Gateway - Volume Gateway 61

AWS Storage Gateway - Tape Gateway 61

Docker Containers and ECS 62

Amazon ECS Key Features 62

Amazon ECS Components 62

ECS Launch Types 62

ECS Images 63

ECS Tasks 63

ECS Clusters 64

ECS Container Agent 64

    Auto Scaling for ECS 64

    Amazon EKS Use Cases 65

    Amazon ECS vs EKS 66

Serverless Applications 67

    Serverless Services 67

    AWS Lambda 67

    Lambda Function Invocations 68

    Application Integration Services Overview 68

    Kinesis vs SQS vs SNS 69

    SQS Queue Types 70

    SQS – Dead Letter Queue 71

    SQS Long Polling vs Short Polling 71

    Amazon SNS 71

    Amazon SNS + Amazon SQS Fan-Out 72

    AWS Step Functions 72

    Amazon EventBridge 72

    API Gateway 73

    API Gateway - Caching 73

    API Gateway - Throttling 73

Databases and Analytics 75

    AWS Databases 75

    Amazon RDS 75

    Amazon RDS 76

    Amazon RDS Multi-AZ and Read Replicas 76

    Amazon RDS Manual Backups (Snapshot) 77

    Amazon RDS Maintenance Windows 77

    Amazon RDS Security 77

    Amazon RDS Security 78

    Amazon Aurora 78

Amazon Aurora Key Features 78
Amazon Aurora Replicas 79
Aurora Serverless Use Cases 80
When NOT to use Amazon RDS (anti-patterns) 80
When NOT to use Amazon RDS (anti-patterns) 80
Database on Amazon EC2 81
Amazon ElastiCache 81
Amazon ElastiCache 81
Amazon ElastiCache Use Cases 82
Amazon DynamoDB 82
Amazon DynamoDB 82
DynamoDB Time to Live (TTL) 83
Amazon DynamoDB 83
DynamoDB Streams 84
DynamoDB Accelerator (DAX) 84
DAX vs ElastiCache 85
RedShift Use Cases 85
Amazon EMR 85
Amazon Kinesis Data Streams 85
Kinesis Client Library (KCL) 86
Kinesis Data Firehose 86
Kinesis Data Firehose 86
Kinesis Data Analytics 87
Amazon Athena 87
Optimizing Athena for Performance 87
AWS Glue 88
AWS Glue 88

Deployment and Management 89

AWS CloudFormation 89

AWS CloudFormation 89

AWS Elastic Beanstalk 89

Web Servers and Workers 90

AWS SSM Parameter Store 90

AWS Config 91

AWS Secrets Manager 91

AWS Secrets Manager vs SSM Parameter Store 91

AWS OpsWorks 92

AWS RAM 92

Monitoring, Logging, and Auditing 94

Amazon CloudWatch 94

Amazon CloudWatch Metrics 94

Amazon CloudWatch Alarms 95

Amazon CloudWatch Logs 95

The Unified CloudWatch Agent 95

AWS CloudTrail 96

CloudTrail – Types of Events 96

Security in the Cloud 97

AWS Managed Microsoft AD 97

AD Connector 97

Simple AD 97

Identity Providers and Federation 98

AWS Single Sign-On 98

Amazon Cognito 98

AWS Key Management Service (KMS) 99

Customer Master Keys (CMKs) 99

AWS Managed CMKs 99

Data Encryption Keys 100

Customer Master Keys (CMKs) 100

AWS CloudHSM 100

AWS CloudHSM Use Cases 101

AWS CloudHSM vs KMS 101

AWS Certificate Manager (ACM) 101

AWS WAF 102

AWS Shield 103

Migration and Transfer Services **105**

AWS Server Migration Service (SMS) 105

AWS Database Migration Service (DMS) 105

AWS DMS Use Cases 105

AWS DataSync 106

AWS Snowball Family 106

AWS Snowball Use Cases 107

Conclusion **108**

Assess your Exam Readiness with Practice Exams 108

Reach Out and Connect 108

How to Access your Video Course 108

Leave us a Review 109

Live Bootcamps and on-demand training **110**

Cloud Mastery Bootcamp (virtual classroom) 110

On-demand / self-paced AWS Training 111

ABOUT THE AUTHOR **112**

Connect with us on Social Media 113

GETTING STARTED

Your Pathway to Success

1: BUILD FOUNDATIONAL KNOWLEDGE
2: ASSESS YOUR EXAM READINESS
3: REVIEW KEY FACTS
4: ACE YOUR EXAM

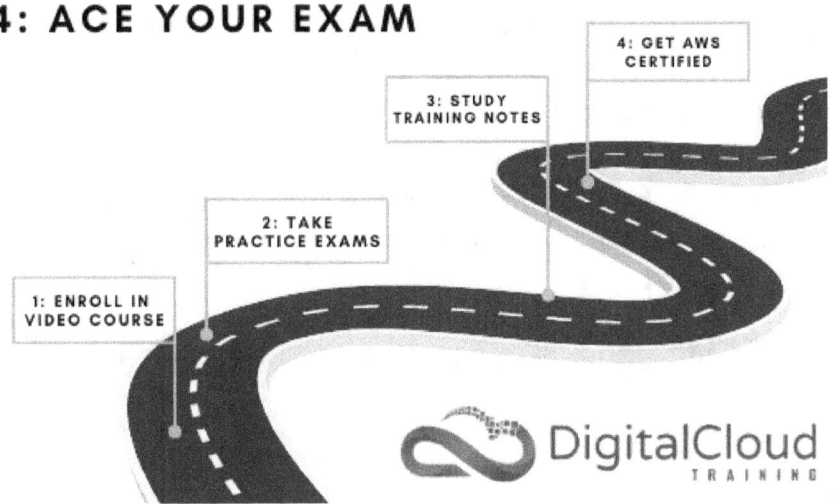

Step 1: Enroll in the Instructor-led Video Course (free of charge)

Congratulations on launching your AWS certification journey and taking the first step towards your exam success. To get started, navigate to the conclusion at the back of the book for detailed instructions on how to enroll in your online course.

Suitable for Beginners to the Cloud

This popular video course is suitable for AWS beginners, as we start with the basics of setting up an account. Using a process of repetition and incremental learning, the course helps you build both practical skills and theoretical knowledge.

How to best use this "exam cram" document

An exam cram is a summary of all the important facts that you need to know for the exam. This document provides a condensed list of facts, backed by tables to help with understanding. There's no need to take additional notes unless you prefer to.

Please note that this document does not read like a traditional book or instructional text.

It's designed as a supplementary learning tool, offering an efficient way to review essential facts. For a deeper understanding of each topic, refer to the video course, which is available online at no additional charge. This document perfectly complements the course, giving you everything you need to succeed in your AWS certification journey.

Step 2: Practice Exam Course with online Exam Simulator

If you are looking for a way to assess your exam readiness, enroll in the practice exam course from Digital Cloud Training. The online exam simulator offers over 500 unique questions, helping you identify your strengths and weaknesses. These practice tests closely mirror the style and difficulty of the actual AWS exam, providing an authentic exam experience.

To learn more, visit https://digitalcloud.training/aws-certified-solutions-architect-associate/

Step 3: Training Notes

As the final step, use these Training Notes for the **AWS Certified Solutions Architect Associate** to focus your studies on the knowledge areas where you need the most improvement. Gain an in-depth understanding of the AWS services and dive deep into the SAA-C03 exam objectives with detailed facts, tables and diagrams.

Cloud Mastery Bootcamp

Did you know that Digital Cloud Training offers remote live training to help you achieve your cloud career goals? The Cloud Mastery Bootcamp is designed to fast-track your cloud career through structured, hands-on training, and comprehensive support.

The Cloud Mastery Bootcamp offers direct access to expert instructors, personalized career guidance, and real-world projects - everything you need to develop job-ready skills for your next-level cloud role. Explore the Cloud Mastery Bootcamp to see if it's the right fit for your career goals: https://digitalcloud.training/cloud-mastery-bootcamp/

Contact, Support & Feedback

We aim to provide you with a 5-star learning experience and ensure you get the most value from these training resources. If for any reason you are not 100% satisfied, please contact us at support@digitalcloud.training. We promise to address all questions and concerns, typically within 24 hours.

The AWS platform is evolving quickly, and the exam tracks these changes with a typical lag of around 6 months. Your feedback plays a crucial role in helping us keep our resources aligned with the latest exam content. If you encounter topics on your exam that weren't covered in our training resources, please share your feedback. We appreciate your input that will help us further improve our AWS training resources. https://digitalcloud.training/student-feedback/.

Reviews Really Matter

If you enjoy reading reviews, please consider paying it forward. Reviews guide students and allow us to continually improve our courses. We value every honest review and truly appreciate your feedback. We'd be thrilled if you could leave us a rating at amazon.com/ryp or your local amazon store (e.g. amazon.co.uk/ryp).

Connect with the AWS Community

Connect with fellow learners and AWS professionals by joining our private LinkedIn group 'AWS Certification & Training' - a great space to ask questions, share knowledge, and exchange exam tips with the AWS community. To join the discussion about all things related to AWS on Slack, visit: http://digitalcloud.training/slack for instructions.

CONNECT WITH US ON SOCIAL MEDIA

Stay updated and engage with us on your favorite platforms. All Links available on https://digitalcloud.training/about-neal-davis-and-digital-cloud-training/

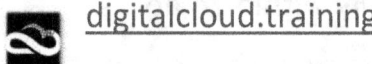 digitalcloud.training

 youtube.com/c/digitalcloudtraining

 facebook.com/digitalcloudtraining

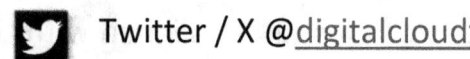 Twitter / X @digitalcloudt

linkedin.com/company/digitalcloudtraining

Instagram @digitalcloudtraining

THE SAA-C03 EXAM VERSION

To help you prepare for the **AWS Certified Solutions Architect Associate** exam, let's take a closer look at the exam blueprint and break down the various "domains" of the exam guide so you know exactly what to expect.

The AWS Certified Solutions Architect Associate exam is recommended for individuals with at least one year of hands-on experience. The exam is intended for Solutions Architects and requires you to demonstrate knowledge of how to define a solution using architectural design principles based on customer requirements and provide implementation guidance based on best practices to the organization throughout the lifecycle of the project.

In the official Exam Guide for the AWS Certified Solutions Architect, the following **AWS knowledge and experience is recommended:**

- One year of hands-on experience with AWS technology, including using compute, networking, storage, and database AWS services as well as AWS deployment and management services
- Experience deploying, managing, and operating workloads on AWS as well as implementing security controls and compliance requirements
- Familiarity with using both the AWS Management Console and the AWS Command Line Interface (CLI)
- Understanding of the AWS Well-Architected Framework, AWS networking, security services, and the AWS global infrastructure
- Ability to identify which AWS services meet a given technical requirement and to define technical requirements for an AWS-based application

The exam includes 65 questions and has a time limit of 130 minutes. You need to score a minimum of 720 out of 1000 points to pass the exam (the pass mark is 72%).

The question format of the exam is multiple-choice (one correct response from four options) and multiple response (two or more correct responses from five or more options). The questions are 100% scenario based with most scenarios being just a couple to a few lines long.

You will find that there are often multiple correct answers, and you must select the answer that best fits the scenario. For instance, you may be asked to select the MOST secure, MOST cost-effective, BEST architecture or LEAST complex option.

Important: Be very careful reading the wording of the question to ensure you select correctly. Sometimes small details can be easily missed that change the answer so take your time when sitting the exam.

Test Domains and Objectives

The knowledge required is organized into four test "domains". Within each test domain, there are several objectives that broadly describe the knowledge and experience required to pass the exam.

Test Domain 1: Design Secure Architectures

This domain makes up 30% of the exam and includes the following four objectives:

1.1 Design secure access to AWS resources.

1.2 Design secure workloads and applications.

1.3 Determine appropriate data security controls.

Test Domain 2: Design Resilient Architectures

This domain makes up 26% of the exam and includes the following **objectives**:

2.1 Design scalable and loosely coupled architectures.

2.2 Design highly available and/or fault-tolerant architectures.

Test Domain 3: Design High-Performing Architectures

This domain makes up 24% of the exam and includes the following objectives:

3.1 Determine high-performing and/or scalable storage solutions.

3.2: Design high-performing and elastic compute solutions.

3.3: Determine high-performing database solutions.

3.4: Determine high-performing and/or scalable network architectures.

3.5: Determine high-performing data ingestion and transformation solutions.

Test Domain 4: Design Cost-Optimized Architectures

This domain makes up 20% of the exam and includes the following objectives:

4.1 Design cost-optimized storage solutions.

4.2: Design cost-optimized compute solutions.

4.3: Design cost-optimized database solutions.

4.4: Design cost-optimized network architectures.

ABOUT EXAM CRAMS

Exam crams are a fast and efficient way to review important facts – perfect for last-minute exam cramming.

However, please note that exam crams are not a substitute for our comprehensive on-demand video course, where Neal provides in-depth explanations of the theory you need to understand to pass your AWS exam. Instead, think of exam crams as a revision tool, designed to remind you of the key facts you need to know for your exam.

These exam crams are intended to supplement the video course, which covers all the content necessary to confidently pass your exam. The video course also features hands-on practical exercises to help you develop valuable cloud skills that go beyond the exam.

Happy learning, and best of luck on your AWS certification journey!

AWS IDENTITY AND ACCESS MANAGEMENT (IAM)

AWS Identity and Access Management (AWS IAM)

IAM is used to securely control individual and group access to AWS resources

IAM makes it easy to provide multiple users secure access to AWS resources

IAM can be used to manage:

- Users
- Groups
- Access policies
- Roles
- User credentials
- User password policies
- Multi-factor authentication (MFA)
- API keys for programmatic access (CLI)

By default, new users are created with NO access to any AWS services – they can only login to the AWS console

Permission must be explicitly granted to allow a user to access an AWS service

IAM users are individuals who have been granted access to an AWS account

IAM is universal (global) and does not apply to regions

IAM is eventually consistent

Authentication methods:

- Console password – use to login to AWS Management Console
- Access keys – used for programmatic access
- Server certificates – uses SSL/TLS certificates

IAM Users

An IAM user is an entity that represents a person or service

By default, users cannot access anything in your account

Root user credentials are the email address used to create the account and a password

The root account has full administrative permissions, and these cannot be restricted

IAM users can be created to represent applications, and these are known as "service accounts"

You can have up to 5000 users per AWS account

IAM Groups

Groups are collections of users and have policies attached to them

A group is not an identity and cannot be identified as a principal in an IAM policy

Use groups to assign permissions to users

Use the principal of least privilege when assigning permissions

You cannot nest groups (groups within groups)

IAM Roles

Roles are created and then "assumed" by trusted entities

With IAM Roles you can delegate permissions to resources for users and services

IAM users or AWS services can assume a role to obtain temporary security credentials

Temporary security credentials are issued by the AWS Security Token Service (STS)

IAM Policies

Policies are documents that define permissions and can be applied to users, groups and roles

Policy documents are written in JSON (key value pair that consists of an attribute and a value)

All permissions are implicitly denied by default

The most restrictive policy is applied

Types of IAM Policy

- **Identity-based policies** – attached to users, groups, or roles
- **Resource-based policies** – attached to a resource; define permissions for a principal accessing the resource
- **IAM permissions boundaries** – set the maximum permissions an identity-based policy can grant an IAM entity
- **AWS Organizations service control policies (SCP)** – specify the maximum permissions for an organization or OU
- **Session policies** – used with AssumeRole API actions

AWS IAM Best Practices

- Lock away your AWS account root user access keys
- Create individual IAM users
- Use groups to assign permissions to IAM users
- Grant least privilege
- Get started using permissions with AWS managed policies
- Use customer managed policies instead of inline policies
- Use access levels to review IAM permissions
- Configure a strong password policy for your users
- Enable MFA
- Use roles for applications that run on Amazon EC2 instances
- Use roles to delegate permissions
- Do not share access keys
- Rotate credentials regularly
- Remove unnecessary credentials
- Use policy conditions for extra security
- Monitor activity in your AWS account

AMAZON ELASTIC COMPUTE CLOUD (EC2)

Amazon EC2

With Amazon EC2 you launch virtual server instances on the AWS cloud

Each virtual server is known as an "instance"

With EC2 you have full control at the operating system layer

Key pairs are used to securely connect to EC2 instances

Storage is either Amazon EBS (persistent) or Instance Store (non-persistent)

An Amazon Machine Image (AMI) provides the information required to launch an instance

An AMI includes the following:

- A template for the root volume for the instance
- Launch permissions
- A block device mapping specifying the volumes to attach

AMIs are regional. You can only launch an AMI from the region in which it is stored

You can copy AMI's to other regions using the console, command line, or the API

Instance metadata is data about your instance that you can use to configure or manage the running instance

User data is data that is supplied by the user at instance launch in the form of a script

Instance metadata is available at http://169.254.169.254/latest/meta-data/

Instance user data is available at: http://169.254.169.254/latest/user-data

Benefits of Amazon EC2

- **Elastic computing** – easily launch hundreds to thousands of EC2 instances within minutes
- **Complete control** – you control the EC2 instances with full root/administrative access

- **Flexible** – Choice of instance types, operating systems, and software packages
- **Reliable** – EC2 offers very high levels of availability and instances can be rapidly commissioned and replaced
- **Secure** – Fully integrated with Amazon VPC and security features
- **Inexpensive** – Low cost, pay for what you use

Public, Private and Elastic IP addresses

Name	Description
Public IP address	Lost when the instance is stopped Used in Public Subnets No charge Associated with a private IP address on the instance Cannot be moved between instances
Private IP address	Retained when the instance is stopped Used in Public and Private Subnets
Elastic IP address	Static Public IP address You are charged if not used Associated with a private IP address on the instance Can be moved between instances and Elastic Network Adapters

EC2 Placement Groups

Cluster – packs instances close together inside an Availability Zone. This strategy enables workloads to achieve the low-latency network performance necessary for tightly-coupled node-to-node communication that is typical of HPC applications

Partition – spreads your instances across logical partitions such that groups of instances in one partition do not share the underlying hardware with groups of instances in different partitions. This strategy is typically used by large distributed and replicated workloads, such as Hadoop, Cassandra, and Kafka

Spread – strictly places a small group of instances across distinct underlying hardware to reduce correlated failures

NAT Instance vs NAT Gateway

NAT Instance	NAT Gateway
Managed by you (e.g. software updates)	Managed by AWS
Scale up (instance type) manually and use enhanced networking	Elastic scalability up to 45 Gbps
No high availability – scripted/auto-scaled HA possible using multiple NATs in multiple subnets	Provides automatic high availability within an AZ and can be placed in multiple AZs
Need to assign Security Group	No Security Groups
Can use as a bastion host	Cannot access through SSH
Use an Elastic IP address or a public IP address with a NAT instance	Choose the Elastic IP address to associate with a NAT gateway at creation
Can implement port forwarding through manual customisation	Does not support port forwarding

EC2 Instance Lifecycle

Stopping EC2 instances

EBS backed instances only

No charge for stopped instances

EBS volumes remain attached (chargeable)

Data in RAM is lost

Instance is migrated to a different host

Private IPv4 addresses and IPv6 addresses retained; public IPv4 addresses released

Associated Elastic IPs retained

Hibernating EC2 instances

Applies to on-demand or reserved Linux instances

Contents of RAM saved to EBS volume

Must be enabled for hibernation when launched

Specific prerequisites apply

When started (after hibernation):

- The EBS root volume is restored to its previous state
- The RAM contents are reloaded
- The processes that were previously running on the instance are resumed
- Previously attached data volumes are reattached and the instance retains its instance ID

Rebooting EC2 instances

- Equivalent to an OS reboot
- DNS name and all IPv4 and IPv6 addresses retained
- Does not affect billing

Retiring EC2 instances

- Instances may be retired if AWS detects irreparable failure of the underlying hardware that hosts the instance
- When an instance reaches its scheduled retirement date, it is stopped or terminated by AWS

Terminating EC2 instances

- Means deleting the EC2 instance
- Cannot recover a terminated instance
- By default root EBS volumes are deleted

Recovering EC2 instances

- CloudWatch can be used to monitor system status checks and recover instance if needed
- Applies if the instance becomes impaired due to underlying hardware / platform issues
- Recovered instance is identical to original instance

AWS Nitro System

Nitro is the underlying platform for the next generation of EC2 instances

Breaks logical functions into specialized hardware with a Nitro Hypervisor

Specialized hardware includes:

- Nitro cards for VPC
- Nitro cards for EBS
- Nitro for Instance Storage
- Nitro card controller
- Nitro security chip
- Nitro hypervisor
- Nitro Enclaves

Improves performance, security and innovation:

- Performance close to bare metal for virtualized instances
- Elastic Network Adapter and Elastic Fabric Adapter
- More bare metal instance types
- Higher network performance (e.g. 100 Gbps)
- High Performance Computing (HPC) optimizations
- Dense storage instances (e.g. 60 TB)

AWS Nitro Enclaves

Isolated compute environments

Runs on isolated and hardened virtual machines

No persistent storage, interactive access, or external networking

Uses cryptographic attestation to ensure only authorized code is running

Integrates with AWS Key Management Service (KMS)

Protect and securely process highly sensitive data:

- Personally identifiable information (PII)
- Healthcare data
- Financial data
- Intellectual Property data

Amazon EC2 Pricing Options

On-Demand

- Standard rate - no discount
- no commitments
- dev/test, short-term, or unpredictable workloads

Spot Instances

- Low price for unused capacity
- up to 90% discount
- can be terminated at any time
- workloads with flexible start and end times

Dedicated Hosts

- Physical server dedicated for your use
- Socket/core visibility, host affinity; pay per host
- workloads with server-bound software licenses

Reserved

- 1 or 3-year commitment
- up to 75% discount
- steady-state, predictable workloads and reserved capacity

Dedicated Instances

- Physical isolation at the host hardware level from instances belonging to other customers; pay per instance

Savings Plans

- Commitment to a consistent amount of usage (EC2 + Fargate + Lambda); Pay by $/hour; 1 or 3-year commitment

Dedicated Instances and Dedicated Hosts

Characteristic	Dedicated Instances	Dedicated Hosts
Enables the use of dedicated physical servers	X	X
Per instance billing (subject to a $2 per region fee)	X	
Per host billing		X
Visibility of sockets, cores, host ID		X
Affinity between a host and instance		X
Targeted instance placement		X
Automatic instance placement	X	X
Add capacity using an allocation request		X

ELASTIC LOAD BALANCING, AND AUTO SCALING

Amazon EC2 Auto Scaling

EC2 Auto Scaling launches and terminates instances dynamically

Scaling is horizontal (scales out)

Provides elasticity and scalability

Responds to EC2 status checks and CloudWatch metrics

Can scale based on demand (performance) or on a schedule

Scaling policies define how to respond to changes in demand

Auto Scaling groups define collections of EC2 instances that are scaled and managed together

Health checks

- EC2 = EC2 status checks
- ELB = Uses the ELB health checks in addition to EC2 status checks

Health check grace period

- How long to wait before checking the health status of the instance
- Auto Scaling does not act on health checks until grace period expires

Auto Scaling - Monitoring

Group metrics (ASG)

- Data points about the Auto Scaling group
- 1-minute granularity
- No charge
- Must be enabled

Basic monitoring (Instances)

- 5-minute granularity
- No Charge

Detailed monitoring (Instances)

- 1-minute granularity
- Charges apply

Additional Scaling Settings

Cooldowns – Used with simple scaling policy to prevent Auto Scaling from launching or terminating before effects of previous activities are visible. Default value is 300 seconds (5 minutes)

Termination Policy – Controls which instances to terminate first when a scale-in event occurs

Termination Protection – Prevents Auto Scaling from terminating protected instances

Standby State – Used to put an instance in the InService state into the Standby state, update or troubleshoot the instance

Lifecycle Hooks – Used to perform custom actions by pausing instances as the ASG launches or terminates them

Use case:

- Run a script to download and install software after launching
- Pause an instance to process data before a scale-in (termination)

Elastic Load Balancing

Distributes incoming application traffic across multiple targets including:

- Amazon EC2 instances
- Containers
- IP addresses
- Lambda functions

Provides fault tolerance for applications

Distributes incoming traffic a single AZ or multiple AZs

Only 1 subnet per AZ can be enabled for each ELB

Ensure at least a /27 subnet and make sure there are at least 8 IP addresses available for the ELB to scale

ELBs can be Internet facing or internal-only

Internet facing ELB:

- ELB nodes have public IPs
- Routes traffic to the private IP addresses of the EC2 instances
- Need one public subnet in each AZ where the ELB is defined

Internal only ELB:

- ELB nodes have private IPs
- Routes traffic to the private IP addresses of the EC2 instances

ELB Use Cases

Application Load Balancer

Web applications with L7 routing (HTTP/HTTPS)

Microservices architectures (e.g. Docker containers)

Lambda targets

Network Load Balancer

TCP and UDP based applications

Ultra-low latency

Static IP addresses

VPC endpoint services

Gateway Load Balancer

Layer 3

Listens for all IP packets across all ports

GLB and virtual appliances exchange application traffic using the GENEVE protocol on port 6081

Use with virtual appliances such as:

- Firewalls
- Intrusion detection systems (IDS)
- Intrusion prevention systems (IPS)
- Deep packet inspection systems (DPI)

Cross-Zone Load Balancing

When cross-zone load balancing is enabled:

- Each load balancer node distributes traffic across the registered targets in all enabled Availability Zones

When cross-zone load balancing is disabled:

- Each load balancer node distributes traffic only across the registered targets in its Availability Zone

With Application Load Balancers, cross-zone load balancing is always enabled

With Network Load Balancers and Gateway Load Balancers, cross-zone load balancing is disabled by default

AWS ORGANIZATIONS

AWS organizations allows you to consolidate multiple AWS accounts into an organization that you create and centrally manage

Available in two feature sets:

- Consolidated Billing
- All features

Includes root accounts and organizational units

Policies are applied to root accounts or OUs

Consolidated billing includes:

- Paying Account – independent and cannot access resources of other accounts
- Linked Accounts – all linked accounts are independent

Consolidated Billing

Single payment method for all the AWS accounts in the Organization

Combined view of charges incurred by all your accounts

Pricing benefits from aggregated usage

Limit of 20 linked accounts for consolidated billing (default)

Can help with cost control through volume discounts

Unused reserved EC2 instances are applied across the group

Paying accounts should be used for billing purposes only

Service Control Policies

Manage the maximum available permissions

Must have all features enabled in Organization

Can be applied to accounts or OUs

Policies can be assigned at different points in the hierarchy

SCPs affect only IAM users and roles – not resources policies

SCPs affect the root account in member accounts

SCPs do not affect any action performed by the management account

Deny list strategy:

- Uses the FullAWSAccess SCP
- Attached to every OU and account
- Overrides the implicit deny
- Explicitly allows all permissions to flow down from the root
- Create additional SCPs to explicitly deny permissions

Allow list strategy:

- FullAWSAccess SCP is removed
- No APIs are permitted anywhere unless you explicitly allow them
- Create SCPs to allow permissions
- SCPs must be attached to target account and every OU above it including root

AWS Organizations - Migration

Accounts can be migrated between organizations

You must have root or IAM access to both the member and management accounts

Use the AWS Organizations console for just a few accounts

Use the AWS Organizations API or AWS CLI if there are many accounts to migrate

AMAZON VIRTUAL PRIVATE CLOUD (VPC)

Amazon VPC

Analogous to having your own DC inside AWS

Provides complete control over the virtual networking environment

A VPC is logically isolated from other VPCs on AWS

VPCs are region wide

A default VPC is created in each region with a subnet in each AZ

By default, you can create up to 5 VPCs per region

Public subnets are subnets that have:

- "Auto-assign public IPv4 address" set to "Yes"
- The subnet route table has an attached Internet Gateway

When you create a VPC, you must specify a range of IPv4 addresses for the VPC in the form of a CIDR block

A VPC spans all the Availability Zones in the region

You have full control over who has access to the AWS resources inside your VPC

AZs names are mapped to different zones for different users – use AZ ID to identify physical zones

Amazon VPC Components

Subnet: A segment of a VPC's IP address range where you can place groups of isolated resources (maps to a single AZ)

Internet Gateway: The Amazon VPC side of a connection to the public Internet

NAT Gateway: A highly available, managed Network Address Translation (NAT) service for your resources in a private subnet to access the Internet

Router: Routers interconnect subnets and direct traffic between Internet gateways, virtual private gateways, NAT gateways, and subnets

Peering Connection: A peering connection enables you to route traffic via private IP addresses between two peered VPCs

VPC Endpoints: Enables private connectivity to services hosted in AWS

Egress-only Internet Gateway: A stateful gateway to provide egress only access for IPv6 traffic from the VPC to the Internet

Hardware VPN Connection: A hardware-based VPN connection between your Amazon VPC and your datacenter, home network, or co-location facility

Virtual Private Gateway: The Amazon VPC side of a VPN connection.

Customer Gateway: Your side of a VPN connection

Rules and Guidelines (IP CIDR)

CIDR block size can be between /16 and /28

The CIDR block must not overlap with any existing CIDR block that's associated with the VPC

You cannot increase or decrease the size of an existing CIDR block

The first four and last IP address are not available for use

AWS recommend you use CIDR blocks from the RFC 1918 ranges

Additional Considerations

Ensure you have enough networks and hosts

Bigger CIDR blocks are typically better (more flexibility)

Smaller subnets are OK for most use cases

Consider deploying application tiers per subnet

Split your HA resources across subnets in different AZs

VPC Peering requires non-overlapping CIDR blocks

- This is across all VPCs in all Regions / accounts you want to connect

Avoid overlapping CIDR blocks as much as possible!

Security Groups vs Network ACLs

Security Group	Network ACL
Operates at the instance level	Operates at the subnet level

© 2026 Digital Cloud Training

Supports allow rules only	Supports allow and deny rules
Stateful	Stateless
Evaluates all rules	Processes rules in order
Applies to an instance only if associated with a group	Automatically applies to all instances in the subnets its associated with

VPC Connectivity – AWS Managed VPN

What	AWS Managed IPSec VPN Connection over your existing Internet
When	Quick and usually simple way to establish a secure tunnelled connection to a VPC; redundant link for Direct Connect or other VPC VPN
Pros	Supports static routes or BGP peering and routing
Cons	Dependent on your Internet connection
How	Create a Virtual Private Gateway (VGW) on AWS, and a Customer Gateway on the on-premises side

VPC Connectivity – AWS Direct Connect

What	Dedicated network connection over private lines straight into the AWS backbone
When	Requires a large network link into AWS; lots of resources and services being provided on AWS to your corporate users
Pros	Predictable network performance; potential bandwidth cost reduction; up to 10/100 Gbps provisioned connections; supports BGP peering and routing

Cons	May require additional telecom and hosting provider relationships and/or network circuits; costly; takes time to provision
How	Work with your existing data networking provider; create Virtual Interfaces (VIFs) to connect to VPCs (private VIFs) or other AWS services like S3 or Glacier (public VIFs)

VPC Connectivity – DX + VPN

What	IPSec VPN connection over private lines (Direct Connect)
When	Need the added security of encrypted tunnels over Direct Connect
Pros	More secure (in theory) than Direct Connect alone
Cons	More complexity introduced by VPN layer
How	Work with your existing data networking provider

VPC Connectivity – VPN CloudHub

What	Connect locations in a hub and spoke manner using AWSs Virtual Private Gateway
When	Link remote offices for backup or primary WAN access to AWS resources and each other
Pros	Reuses existing Internet connections; supports BGP routes to direct traffic
Cons	Dependent on Internet connection; no inherent redundancy
How	Assign multiple Customer Gateways to a Virtual Private Gateway, each with their own BGP ASN and unique IP ranges

VPC Connectivity – Software VPN

What	You provide your own VPN endpoint and software
When	You must manage both ends of the VPN connection for compliance reasons or you want to use a VPN option not supported by AWS
Pros	Ultimate flexibility and manageability
Cons	You must design for any needed redundancy across the whole chain
How	Install VPN software via Marketplace appliance of on an EC2 instance

VPC Connectivity – Transit VPC

What	Common strategy for connecting geographically dispersed VPCs and locations in order to create a global network transit center
When	Locations and VPC-deployed assets across multiple regions that need to communicate with one another
Pros	Ultimate flexibility and manageability but also AWS-managed VPN hub-and-spoke between VPCs
Cons	You must design for any needed redundancy across the whole chain
How	Providers like Cisco, Juniper Networks, and Riverbed have offerings which work with their equipment and AWS VPC

VPC Connectivity – VPC Peering

What	AWS-provided network connectivity between two VPCs
When	Multiple VPCs need to communicate or access each other's resources
Pros	Uses AWS backbone without traversing the Internet

Cons	Transitive peering is not supported
How	VPC peering request made; accepter accepts request (either within or across accounts)

VPC Connectivity – VPC Endpoints

	Interface Endpoint	Gateway Endpoint
What	Elastic Network Interface with a Private IP	A gateway that is a target for a specific route
How	Uses DNS entries to redirect traffic	Uses prefix lists in the route table to redirect traffic
Which services	API Gateway, CloudFormation, CloudWatch etc.	Amazon S3, DynamoDB
Security	Security Groups	VPC Endpoint Policies

VPC Flow Logs

Flow Logs capture information about the IP traffic going to and from network interfaces in a VPC

Flow log data is stored using Amazon CloudWatch Logs or S3

Flow logs can be created at the following levels:

- VPC
- Subnet
- Network interface

AMAZON SIMPLE STORAGE SERVICE (S3)

You can store any type of file in S3

Files can be anywhere from 0 bytes to 5 TB

There is unlimited storage available

S3 is a universal namespace so bucket names must be unique globally

However, you create your buckets within a REGION

It is a best practice to create buckets in regions that are physically closest to your users to reduce latency

There is no hierarchy for objects within a bucket

Delivers strong read-after-write consistency

S3 Buckets

Files are stored in buckets

A bucket can be viewed as a container for objects

A bucket is a flat container of objects

It does not provide a hierarchy of objects

You can use an object key name (prefix) to mimic folders

100 buckets per account by default

You can store unlimited objects in your buckets

You cannot create nested buckets

S3 Objects

An object is a file uploaded to S3

S3 supports any file type

Each object is stored and retrieved by a unique key

Objects remain in the region they are stored you setup replication

Permissions can be defined on objects at any time

Storage class is set at the object level

S3 Storage Classes

	S3 Standard	S3 Intelligent Tiering	S3 Standard-IA	S3 One Zone-IA	S3 Glacier	S3 Glacier Deep Archive
Designed for durability	99.99%	99.99%	99.99%	99.99%	99.99%	99.99%
Designed for availability	99.99%	99.9%	99.9%	99.5%	99.99%	99.99%
Availability SLA	99.9%	99%	99%	99%	99.9%	99.9%
Availability Zones	≥ 3	≥ 3	≥ 3	1	≥ 3	≥ 3
Minimum capacity charge per object	N/A	N/A	128KB	128KB	40KB	40KB
Minimum storage duration charge	N/A	30 days	30 days	30 days	90 days	180 days
Retrieval fee	N/A	N/A	Per GB retrieved	Per GB retrieved	Per GB retrieved	Per GB retrieved
First byte latency	milliseconds	milliseconds	milliseconds	milliseconds	select minutes or hours	select hours
Storage type	Object	Object	Object	Object	Object	Object
Lifecycle transitions	Yes	Yes	Yes	Yes	Yes	Yes

IAM / Bucket Policies

IAM Policies are identity-based policies

Principal is not defined with an IAM policy

Bucket Policies are resource-based policies

Bucket policies can only be attached to Amazon S3 buckets

Both use the AWS access policy language

S3 Access Control Lists (ACLs)

Legacy access control mechanism that predates IAM

AWS generally recommends using S3 bucket policies or IAM policies rather than ACLs

Can be attached to a bucket or directly to an object

Limited options for grantees and permissions

When to use each access control mechanism

Use IAM policies if:

- You need to control access to AWS services other than S3
- You have numerous S3 buckets each with different permissions requirements (IAM policies will be easier to manage)
- You prefer to keep access control policies in the IAM environment

Use S3 bucket policies if:

- You want a simple way to grant cross-account access to your S3 environment, without using IAM roles
- Your IAM policies are reaching the size limits
- You prefer to keep access control policies in the S3 environment

S3 Versioning

Versioning is a means of keeping multiple variants of an object in the same bucket

Use versioning to preserve, retrieve, and restore every version of every object stored in your Amazon S3 bucket

Versioning-enabled buckets enable you to recover objects from accidental deletion or overwrite

S3 Lifecycle Management

There are two types of actions:

- Transition actions - Define when objects transition to another storage class
- Expiration actions - Define when objects expire (deleted by S3)

S3 LM: Supported Transitions

You can transition from the following:

- The S3 Standard storage class to any other storage class
- Any storage class to the S3 Glacier or S3 Glacier Deep Archive storage classes
- The S3 Standard-IA storage class to the S3 Intelligent-Tiering or S3 One Zone-IA storage classes
- The S3 Intelligent-Tiering storage class to the S3 One Zone-IA storage class
- The S3 Glacier storage class to the S3 Glacier Deep Archive storage class

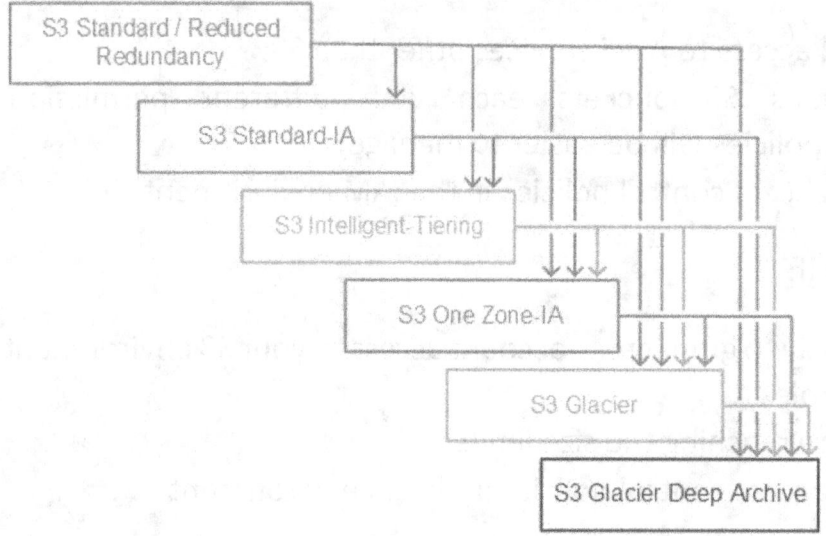

S3 LM: Unsupported Transitions

You can't transition from the following:

- Any storage class to the S3 Standard storage class
- Any storage class to the Reduced Redundancy storage class
- The S3 Intelligent-Tiering storage class to the S3 Standard-IA storage class

- The S3 One Zone-IA storage class to the S3 Standard-IA or S3 Intelligent-Tiering storage classes

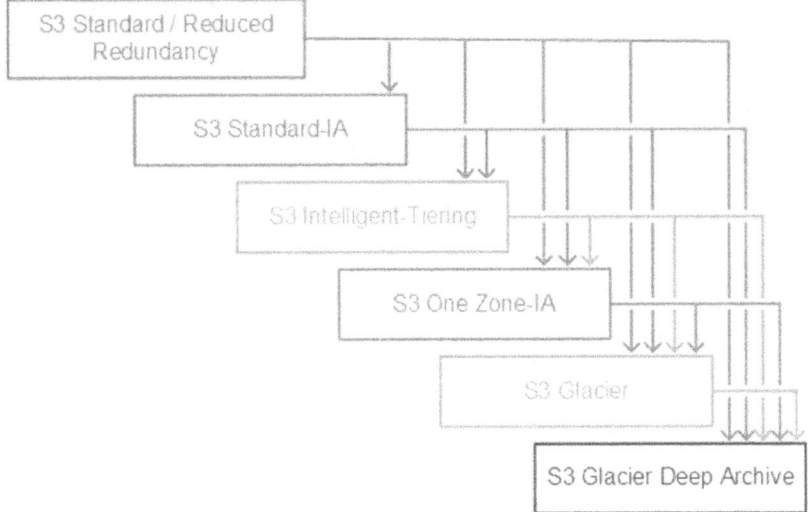

S3 Multi-Factor Authentication Delete (MFA Delete)

Adds MFA requirement for bucket owners to the following operations:

- Changing the versioning state of a bucket
- Permanently deleting an object version

The x-amz-mfa request header must be included in the above requests

The second factor is a token generated by a hardware device or software program

Requires versioning to be enabled on the bucket

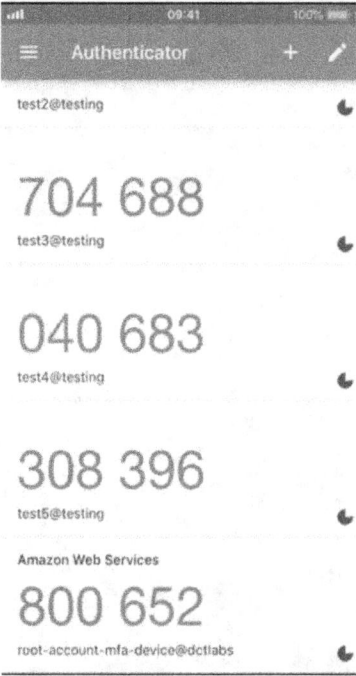

S3 Multi-Factor Authentication Delete (MFA Delete)

Versioning can be enabled by:

- Bucket owners (root account)
- AWS account that created the bucket
- Authorized IAM users

MFA delete can be enabled by:

- Bucket owner (root account)

MFA-Protected API Access

Used to enforce another authentication factor (MFA code) when accessing AWS resources (not just S3)

Enforced using the aws:MultiFactorAuthAge key in a bucket policy:

S3 Encryption

Encryption Option	How it Works
SSE-S3	Use S3's existing encryption key for AES-256

SSE-C	Upload your own AES-256 encryption key which S3 uses when it writes objects
SSE-KMS	Use a key generated and managed by AWS KMS
Client-Side	Encrypt objects using your own local encryption process before uploading to S3

S3 Default Encryption

Amazon S3 default encryption provides a way to set the default encryption behavior for an S3 bucket

You can set default encryption on a bucket so that all new objects are encrypted when they are stored in the bucket

The objects are encrypted using server-side encryption

Amazon S3 encrypts objects before saving them to disk and decrypts them when the objects are downloaded

There is no change to the encryption of objects that existed in the bucket before default encryption was enabled

S3 Event Notifications

Sends notifications when events happen in buckets

Destinations include:

- Amazon Simple Notification Service (SNS) topics
- Amazon Simple Queue Service (SQS) queues
- AWS Lambda

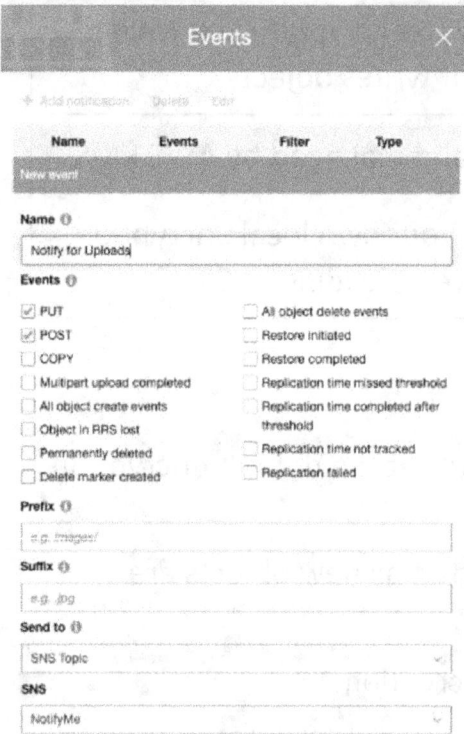

S3 Multipart Upload

Multipart upload uploads objects in parts independently, in parallel and in any order

Performed using the S3 Multipart upload API

It is recommended for objects of 100 MB or larger

Can be used for objects from 5 MB up to 5 TB

Must be used for objects larger than 5 GB

S3 Transfer Acceleration

Enables fast, easy, and secure transfers of files

Leverages Amazon CloudFront Edge Location

Used to accelerate object uploads to S3 over long distances (latency)

Transfer acceleration is as secure as a direct upload to S3

You are charged only if there was a benefit in transfer times

Need to enable transfer acceleration on the S3 bucket

Cannot be disabled, can only be suspended

S3 Copy API

Copy objects up to 5 GB in size

The copy operation can be used to:

- Generate additional copies of objects
- Rename objects
- Change the copy's storage class or encryption at rest status
- Move objects across AWS locations/regions
- Change object metadata

Server Access Logging

Provides detailed records for the requests that are made to a bucket

Details include the requester, bucket name, request time, request action, response status, and error code (if applicable)

Disabled by default

Only pay for the storage space used

Must configure a separate bucket as the destination (can specify a prefix)

Must grant write permissions to the Amazon S3 Log Delivery group on destination bucket

CORS with Amazon S3

Enabled through setting:

- Access-Control-Allow-Origin
- Access-Control-Allow-Methods
- Access-Control-Allow-Headers

These settings are defined using rules

Rules are added using JSON files in S3

Cross Account Access Methods

Resource-based policies and IAM policies for programmatic-only access to S3 bucket objects

Resource-based ACL and IAM policies for programmatic-only access to S3 bucket objects

Cross-account IAM roles for programmatic and console access to S3 bucket objects

S3 Performance Optimizations

S3 supports at least 3,500 PUT/COPY/POST/DELETE or 5,500 GET/HEAD requests per second per prefix in a bucket

Increase read or write performance by parallelizing reads

Use Byte-Range Fetches

Retry Requests for Latency-Sensitive Applications

Combine Amazon S3 (Storage) and Amazon EC2 (Compute) in the Same AWS Region

Use Amazon S3 Transfer Acceleration to Minimize Latency Caused by Distance

DNS, CACHING, AND PERFORMANCE OPTIMIZATION

Amazon Route 53

Route 53 offers the following functions:

- Domain name registry
- DNS resolution
- Health checking of resources

Route 53 is located alongside all edge locations

Route 53 becomes the authoritative DNS server for registered domains and creates a public hosted zone

Private DNS lets you have an authoritative DNS within your VPCs without exposing your DNS records

You can transfer domains to Route 53 only if the Top-Level Domain (TLD) is supported

You can transfer a domain from Route 53 to another registrar by contacting AWS support

You can transfer a domain to another account in AWS (does not migrate zone by default)

Can have a domain registered in one AWS account and the hosted zone in another AWS account

Route 53 Hosted Zones

Collection of records for a specified domain

There are two types of zones:

- Public host zone – determines how traffic is routed on the Internet
- Private hosted zone for VPC – determines how traffic is routed within VPC

For private hosted zones you must set the following VPC settings to "true":

- enableDnsHostname.
- enableDnsSupport

Route 53 Health Checks

Health checks check the instance health by connecting to it

Health checks can be pointed at:

- Endpoints
- Status of other health checks
- Status of a CloudWatch alarm

Endpoints can be IP addresses or domain names

CNAME vs Alias Records

CNAME	Alias
Route 53 charges for CNAME queries	Route 53 doesn't charge for alias queries to AWS resources
You can't create a CNAME record at the top node of a DNS namespace (zone apex)	You can create an alias record at the zone apex (however you can't route to a CNAME at the zone apex)
A CNAME can point to any DNS record that is hosted anywhere	An alias record can only point to a CloudFront distribution, Elastic Beanstalk environment, ELB, S3 bucket as a static website, or to another record in the same hosted zone that you're creating the alias record in

Amazon Route 53 Routing Policies

Routing Policy	What it does
Simple	Simple DNS response providing the IP address associated with a name
Failover	If primary is down (based on health checks), routes to secondary destination
Geolocation	Uses geographic location you're in (e.g. Europe) to route you to the closest region

Geoproximity	Routes you to the closest region within a geographic area
Latency	Directs you based on the lowest latency route to resources
Multivalue answer	Returns several IP addresses and functions as a basic load balancer
Weighted	Uses the relative weights assigned to resources to determine which to route to

Amazon CloudFront Caching

You can define a maximum Time To Live (TTL) and a default TTL

TTL is defined at the behavior level

This can be used to define different TTLs for different file types (e.g. png vs jpg)

After expiration, CloudFront checks the origin for any new requests (check the file is the latest version)

Headers can be used to control the cache:

- Cache-Control max-age=(seconds) - specify how long before CloudFront gets the object again from the origin server
- Expires – specify an expiration date and time

Caching Based on Request Headers

You can configure CloudFront to forward headers in the viewer request to the origin

CloudFront can then cache multiple versions of an object based on the values in one or more request headers

Controlled in a behavior to do one of the following:

- Forward all headers to your origin (objects are not cached)
- Forward a whitelist of headers that you specify
- Forward only the default headers (doesn't cache objects based on values in request headers)

CloudFront Signed URLs / Cookies

Signed URLs

- Signed URLs provide more control over access to content.
- Can specify beginning and expiration date and time, IP addresses/ranges of users

Signed Cookies

- Similar to Signed URLs
- Use signed cookies when you don't want to change URLs
- Can also be used when you want to provide access to multiple restricted files (Signed URLs are for individual files)

Lambda@Edge

Run Node.js and Python Lambda functions to customize the content

- CloudFront delivers

Executes functions closer to the viewer

Can be run at the following points

- After CloudFront receives a request from a viewer (viewer request)
- Before CloudFront forwards the request to the origin (origin request)
- After CloudFront receives the response from the origin (origin response)
- Before CloudFront forwards the response to the viewer (viewer response)

BLOCK AND FILE STORAGE

Amazon EBS

EBS volume data persists independently of the life of the instance

EBS volumes do not need to be attached to an instance

You can attach multiple EBS volumes to an instance

You can use multi-attach to attach a volume to multiple instances but with some constraints

EBS volumes must be in the same AZ as the instances they are attached to

Root EBS volumes are deleted on termination by default

Extra non-boot volumes are not deleted on termination by default

Amazon EBS SSD-Backed Volumes

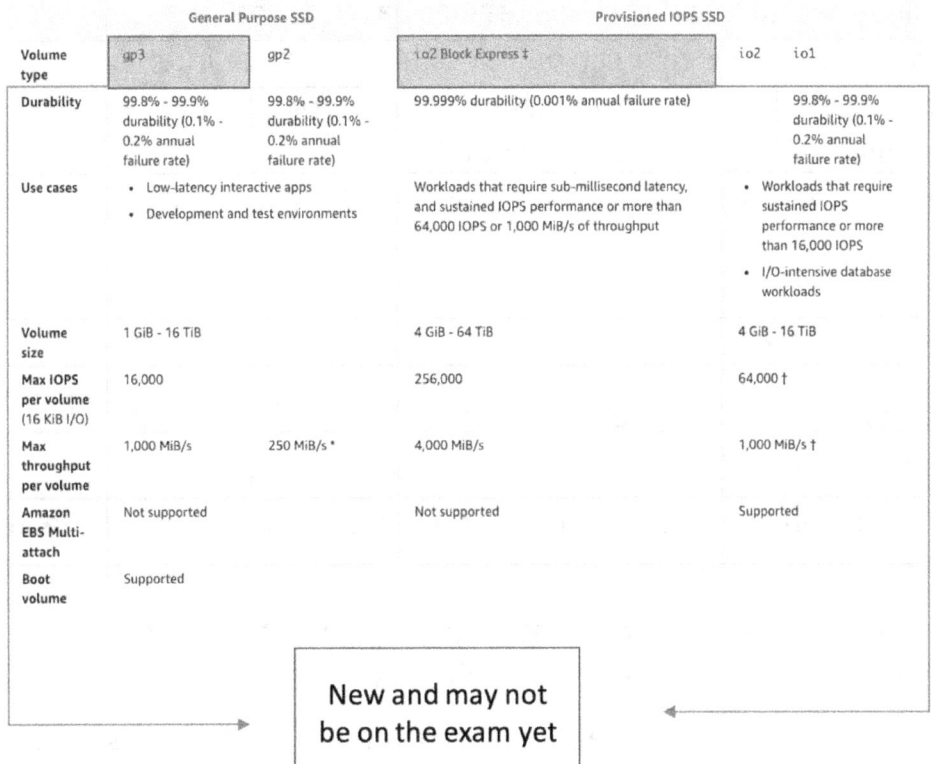

Amazon EBS HDD-Backed Volumes

	Throughput Optimized HDD	Cold HDD
Volume type	st1	sc1
Durability	99.8% - 99.9% durability (0.1% - 0.2% annual failure rate)	99.8% - 99.9% durability (0.1% - 0.2% annual failure rate)
Use cases	<ul><li>Big data</li><li>Data warehouses</li><li>Log processing</li></ul>	<ul><li>Throughput-oriented storage for data that is infrequently accessed</li><li>Scenarios where the lowest storage cost is important</li></ul>
Volume size	125 GiB - 16 TiB	125 GiB - 16 TiB
Max IOPS per volume (1 MiB I/O)	500	250
Max throughput per volume	500 MiB/s	250 MiB/s
Amazon EBS Multi-attach	Not supported	Not supported
Boot volume	Not supported	Not supported

Amazon Data Lifecycle Manager (DLM)

DLM automates the creation, retention, and deletion of EBS snapshots and EBS-backed AMIs

DLM helps with the following:

- Protects valuable data by enforcing a regular backup schedule
- Create standardized AMIs that can be refreshed at regular intervals
- Retain backups as required by auditors or internal compliance
- Reduce storage costs by deleting outdated backups
- Create disaster recovery backup policies that back up data to isolated accounts

EBS vs instance store

Instance store volumes are high performance local disks that are physically attached to the host computer on which an EC2 instance runs

Instance stores are ephemeral which means the data is lost when powered off (non-persistent)

Instance stores are ideal for temporary storage of information that changes frequently, such as buffers, caches, or scratch data

Instance store volume root devices are created from AMI templates stored on S3

Instance store volumes cannot be detached/reattached

Amazon Machine Images (AMIs)

An Amazon Machine Image (AMI) provides the information required to launch an instance

An AMI includes the following:

- One or more EBS snapshots, or, for instance-store-backed AMIs, a template for the root volume of the instance (for example, an operating system, an application server, and applications)
- Launch permissions that control which AWS accounts can use the AMI to launch instances
- A block device mapping that specifies the volumes to attach to the instance when it's launched

AMIs come in three main categories:

- Community AMIs - free to use, generally you just select the operating system you want
- AWS Marketplace AMIs - pay to use, generally come packaged with additional, licensed software
- My AMIs - AMIs that you create yourself

EBS Snapshots

Snapshots capture a point-in-time state of an instance

Cost-effective and easy backup strategy

Can be used to migrate a system to a new AZ or region

Can be used to convert an unencrypted volume to an encrypted volume

Snapshots are stored on Amazon S3

EBS volumes are AZ specific but snapshots are region specific

Using RAID with EBS

RAID stands for Redundant Array of Independent disks

Not provided by AWS, you must configure through your operating system

RAID 0 and RAID 1 are potential options on EBS

RAID 5 and RAID 6 are not recommended by AWS

RAID 0 is used for striping data across disks (performance):

- Use 2 or more disks
- If one disk fails, the entire RAID set fails

RAID 1 is used for mirroring data across disks (redundancy / fault tolerance):

- If one disk fails, the other disk is still working
- Data gets sent to 2 EBS volumes at the same time

EBS Encryption

You can encrypt both the boot and data volumes of an EC2 instance

The following are encrypted:

- Data at rest inside the volume
- All data moving between the volume and the instance
- All snapshots created from the volume
- All volumes created from those snapshots

Encryption is supported by all EBS volume types

All instance families support encryption

Amazon Elastic File System (EFS)

Fully-managed file system solution

Accessed using the NFS protocol

Elastic storage capacity and pay for what you use

Multi-AZ metadata and data storage

Can configure mount-points in one, or many, AZs

Can be mounted from on-premises systems ONLY if using Direct Connect or a VPN connection

Alternatively, use the AWS DataSync

EFS is elastic and grows and shrinks as you add and remove data

Can scale up to petabytes

Can concurrently connect up to 1000s of EC2 instances, from multiple AZs

Can choose General Purpose or Max I/O (both SSD)

Data is stored across multiple AZ's within a region

Read after write consistency

Need to create mount targets and choose AZ's to include

EFS Access Control

You can control who can administer your file system using IAM

You can control access to files and directories with POSIX-compliant user and group-level permissions

POSIX permissions allow you to restrict access from hosts by user and group

EFS Security Groups act as a firewall, and the rules you add define the traffic flow

EFS Encryption

EFS offers the ability to encrypt data at rest and in transit

Encryption at rest MUST be enabled at file system creation time

Encryption keys are managed by AWS KMS

Data encryption in transit uses industry standard Transport Layer Security (TLS)

AWS DataSync

Provides a fast and simple way to securely sync existing file systems into Amazon EFS

Securely and efficiently copies files over the internet or an AWS Direct Connect connection

Copies file data and file system metadata such as ownership, timestamps, and access permissions

Amazon FSx

Amazon FSx provides fully managed third-party file systems

Amazon FSx provides you with two file systems to choose from:

- Amazon FSx for Windows File Server for Windows-based applications
- Amazon FSx for Lustre for compute-intensive workloads

Amazon FSx for Windows File Server

Provides a fully managed native Microsoft Windows file system

Full support for the SMB protocol, Windows NTFS, and Microsoft Active Directory (AD) integration

Supports Windows-native file system features:

- Access Control Lists (ACLs), shadow copies, and user quotas.
- NTFS file systems that can be accessed from up to thousands of compute instances using the SMB protocol

High availability: replicates data within an Availability Zone (AZ)

Multi-AZ: file systems include an active and standby file server in separate AZs

Amazon FSx for Lustre

High-performance file system optimized for fast processing of workloads such as:

- Machine learning
- High performance computing (HPC)
- Video processing
- Financial modeling
- Electronic design automation (EDA)

Works natively with S3, letting you transparently access your S3 objects as files

Your S3 objects are presented as files in your file system, and you can write your results back to S3

Provides a POSIX-compliant file system interface

AWS Storage Gateway – File Gateway

File gateway provides a virtual on-premises file server

Store and retrieve files as objects in Amazon S3

Use with on-premises applications, and EC2-based applications that need file storage in S3 for object-based workloads

File gateway offers SMB or NFS-based access to data in Amazon S3 with local caching

AWS Storage Gateway - Volume Gateway

The volume gateway supports block-based volumes

Block storage – iSCSI protocol

Cached Volume mode – the entire dataset is stored on S3 and a cache of the most frequently accessed data is cached on-site

Stored Volume mode – the entire dataset is stored on-site and is asynchronously backed up to S3 (EBS point-in-time snapshots). Snapshots are incremental and compressed

AWS Storage Gateway - Tape Gateway

Used for backup with popular backup software

Each gateway is preconfigured with a media changer and tape drives. Supported by NetBackup, Backup Exec, Veeam etc.

When creating virtual tapes, you select one of the following sizes: 100 GB, 200 GB, 400 GB, 800 GB, 1.5 TB, and 2.5 TB

A tape gateway can have up to 1,500 virtual tapes with a maximum aggregate capacity of 1 PB

All data transferred between the gateway and AWS storage is encrypted using SSL

All data stored by tape gateway in S3 is encrypted server-side with Amazon S3-Managed Encryption Keys (SSE-S3)

DOCKER CONTAINERS AND ECS

Amazon ECS Key Features

Serverless with AWS Fargate – managed for you and fully scalable

Fully managed container orchestration – control plane is managed for you

Docker support – run and manage Docker containers with integration into the Docker Compose CLI

Windows container support – ECS supports management of Windows containers

Elastic Load Balancing integration – distribute traffic across containers using ALB or NLB

Amazon ECS Anywhere (NEW) – enables the use of Amazon ECS control plane to manage on-premises implementations

Amazon ECS Components

Elastic Container Service (ECS)	Description
Cluster	Logical grouping of EC2 instances
Container instance	EC2 instance running the the ECS agent
Task Definition	Blueprint that describes how a docker container should launch
Task	A running container using settings in a Task Definition
Service	Defines long running tasks – can control task count with Auto Scaling and attach an ELB

ECS Launch Types

An ECS launch type determines the type of infrastructure on which your tasks and services are hosted

There are two launch types:

Amazon EC2	Amazon Fargate
You explicitly provision EC2 instances	The control plane asks for resources and Fargate automatically provisions
You're responsible for upgrading, patching, care of EC2 pool	Fargate provisions compute as needed
You must handle cluster optimization	Fargate handles cluster optimization
More granular control over infrastructure	Limited control, as infrastructure is automated

ECS Images

Containers are created from a read-only template called an image which has the instructions for creating a Docker container

Images are built from a Dockerfile

Only Docker containers are currently supported

An image contains the instructions for creating a Docker container

Images are stored in a registry such as DockerHub or AWS Elastic Container Registry (ECR)

ECR is a managed AWS Docker registry service that is secure, scalable and reliable

ECS Tasks

A task definition is required to run Docker containers in Amazon ECS

A task definition is a text file in JSON format that describes one or more containers, up to a maximum of 10

Task definitions use Docker images to launch containers

You specify the number of tasks to run (i.e. the number of containers)

ECS Clusters

ECS Clusters are a logical grouping of container instances the you can place tasks on

ECS allows the definition of a specified number (desired count) of tasks to run in the cluster

Clusters can contain tasks using the Fargate and EC2 launch type

Each container instance may only be part of one cluster at a time

You can create IAM policies for your clusters to allow or restrict users' access to specific clusters

ECS Container Agent

The ECS container agent allows container instances to connect to the cluster

The container agent runs on each infrastructure resource on an ECS cluster

The ECS container agent is included in the Amazon ECS optimized AMI

Linux and Windows based

For non-AWS Linux instances to be used on AWS you must manually install the ECS container agent

Auto Scaling for ECS

Two types of scaling:
1. Service auto scaling
2. Cluster auto scaling

Service auto scaling automatically adjusts the desired task count up or down using the Application Auto Scaling service

Service auto scaling supports target tracking, step, and scheduled scaling policies

Cluster auto scaling uses a Capacity Provider to scale the number of EC2 cluster instances using EC2 Auto Scaling

Service Auto Scaling

Amazon ECS Service Auto Scaling supports the following types of scaling policies:

- Target Tracking Scaling Policies—Increase or decrease the number of tasks that your service runs based on a target value for a specific CloudWatch metric
- Step Scaling Policies—Increase or decrease the number of tasks that your service runs in response to CloudWatch alarms. Step scaling is based on a set of scaling adjustments, known as step adjustments, which vary based on the size of the alarm breach
- Scheduled Scaling—Increase or decrease the number of tasks that your service runs based on the date and time

Cluster Auto Scaling

Uses an ECS resource type called a Capacity Provider

A Capacity Provider can be associated with an EC2 Auto Scaling Group (ASG)

ASG can automatically scale using:

- **Managed scaling** - with an automatically-created scaling policy on your ASG
- **Managed instance termination protection** - which enables container-aware termination of instances in the ASG when scale-in happens

Amazon EKS Use Cases

Use when you need to standardize container orchestration across multiple environments using a managed Kubernetes implementation

Hybrid Deployment - manage Kubernetes clusters and applications across hybrid environments (AWS + On-premises)

Batch Processing - run sequential or parallel batch workloads on your EKS cluster using the Kubernetes Jobs API. Plan, schedule and execute batch workloads

Machine Learning - use Kubeflow with EKS to model your machine learning workflows and efficiently run distributed training jobs using the latest EC2 GPU-powered instances, including Inferentia

Web Applications - build web applications that automatically scale up and down and run in a highly available configuration across multiple Availability Zones

Amazon ECS vs EKS

Amazon ECS	Amazon EKS
Managed, highly available, highly scalable container platform	
AWS-specific platform that supports Docker containers	Compatible with upstream Kubernetes so it's easy to lift and shift from other Kubernetes deployments
Considered simpler to learn and use	Considered more feature-rich and complex with a steep learning curve
Leverages AWS services like Route 53, ALB, and CloudWatch	A hosted Kubernetes platform that handles many things internally
"Tasks" are instances of containers that are run on underlying compute but more or less isolated	"Pods" are containers collocated with one another and can have shared access to each other
Limited extensibility	Extensible via a wide variety of third-party and community add-ons

SERVERLESS APPLICATIONS

Serverless Services

With serverless there are no instances to manage

You don't need to provision hardware

There is no management of operating systems or software

Capacity provisioning and patching is handled automatically

Provides automatic scaling and high availability

Can be very cheap!

AWS Lambda

AWS Lambda runs code as "functions"

AWS Lambda executes code only when needed and scales automatically

You pay only for the compute time you consume (you pay nothing when your code is not running)

You specify the amount of memory you need allocated to your Lambda functions

AWS Lambda allocates CPU power proportional to the memory you specify using the same ratio as a general purpose EC2 instance type

There is a maximum execution timeout

- Max is 15 minutes (900 seconds), default is 3 seconds
- Lambda terminates the function at the timeout

Lambda is an event-driven compute service

An event source is an AWS service application that produces events that trigger an AWS Lambda function

Event sources are mapped to Lambda functions

For stream-based services Lambda performs the polling (e.g. DynamoDB or Kinesis)

Benefits of AWS Lambda:

- No servers to manage
- Continuous scaling
- Millisecond billing
- Integrates with almost all other AWS services

Primary use cases for AWS Lambda:

- Data processing
- Real-time file processing
- Real-time stream processing
- Build serverless backends for web, mobile, IOT, and 3rd party API requests

Lambda Function Invocations

Synchronous:

CLI, SDK, API Gateway

Result returned immediately

Error handling happens client side (retries, exponential backoff etc.)

Asynchronous:

S3, SNS, CloudWatch Events etc.

Lambda retries up to 3 times

Processing must be idempotent (due to retries)

> SQS can also **trigger** Lambda

Event source mapping:

SQS, Kinesis Data Streams, DynamoDB Streams

Lambda does the polling (polls the source)

Records are processed in order (except for SQS standard)

Application Integration Services Overview

Service	What it does	Example use cases
Simple Queue Service	Messaging queue; store and forward patterns	Building distributed / decoupled applications

Simple Notification Service	Set up, operate, and send notifications from the cloud	Send email notification when CloudWatch alarm is triggered
Step Functions	Out-of-the-box coordination of AWS service components with visual workflow	Order processing workflow
Simple Workflow Service	Need to support external processes or specialized execution logic	Human-enabled workflows like an order fulfilment system or for procedural requests Note: AWS recommends that for new applications customers consider Step Functions instead of SWF
Amazon MQ	Message broker service for Apache Active MQ and RabbitMQ	Need a message queue that supports industry standard APIs and protocols; migrate queues to AWS
Amazon Kinesis	Collect, process, and analyze streaming data.	Collect data from IoT devices for later processing

Kinesis vs SQS vs SNS

Amazon Kinesis	Amazon SQS	Amazon SNS
Consumers pull data	Consumers pull data	Push data to many subscribers
As many consumers as you need	Data is deleted after being consumed	Publisher / subscriber model
Routes related records to same record processor	Can have as many workers (consumers) as you need	Integrates with SQS for fan-out architecture pattern

Multiple applications can access stream concurrently	No ordering guarantee (except with FIFO queues)	Up to 10,000,000 subscribers
Ordering at the shard level	Provides messaging semantics	Up to 100,000 topics
Can consume records in correct order at later time	Individual message delay	Data is not persisted
Must provision throughput	Dynamically scales	No need to provision throughput

SQS Queue Types

Standard Queue	FIFO Queue
Unlimited Throughput: Standard queues support a nearly unlimited number of transactions per second (TPS) per API action.	High Throughput: FIFO queues support up to 300 messages per second (300 send, receive, or delete operations per second). When you batch 10 messages per operation (maximum), FIFO queues can support up to 3,000 messages per second
Best-Effort Ordering: Occasionally, messages might be delivered in an order different from which they were sent	First-In-First-out Delivery: The order in which messages are sent and received is strictly preserved
At-Least-Once Delivery: A message is delivered at least once, but occasionally more than one copy of a message is delivered	Exactly-Once Processing: A message is delivered once and remains available until a consumer processes and deletes it. Duplicates are not introduced into the queue

FIFO queues require the Message Group ID and Message Deduplication ID parameters to be added to messages

Message Group ID:

- The tag that specifies that a message belongs to a specific message group Messages that belong to the same message group are guaranteed to be processed in a FIFO manner

Message Deduplication ID:

- The token used for deduplication of messages within the deduplication interval

SQS – Dead Letter Queue

The main task of a dead-letter queue is handling message failure

A dead-letter queue lets you set aside and isolate messages that can't be processed correctly to determine why their processing didn't succeed

It is not a queue type, it is a standard or FIFO queue that has been specified as a dead-letter queue in the configuration of another standard or FIFO queue

SQS Long Polling vs Short Polling

SQS Long polling is a way to retrieve messages from SQS queues – waits for messages to arrive

SQS Short polling returns immediately (even if the message queue is empty)

SQS Long polling can lower costs

SQS Long polling can be enabled at the queue level or at the API level using WaitTimeSeconds

SQS Long polling is in effect when the Receive Message Wait Time is a value greater than 0 seconds and up to 20 seconds

Amazon SNS

Amazon SNS is a highly available, durable, secure, fully managed pub/sub messaging service

Amazon SNS provides topics for high-throughput, push-based, many-to-many messaging

Publisher systems can fan out messages to a large number of subscriber endpoints

Endpoints include:
- Amazon SQS queues
- AWS Lambda functions
- HTTP/S webhooks
- Mobile push
- SMS
- Email

Multiple recipients can be grouped using Topics

A topic is an "access point" for allowing recipients to dynamically subscribe for identical copies of the same notification

One topic can support deliveries to multiple endpoint types

Simple APIs and easy integration with applications

Flexible message delivery over multiple transport protocols

Amazon SNS + Amazon SQS Fan-Out

You can subscribe one or more Amazon SQS queues to an Amazon SNS topic

Amazon SQS manages the subscription and any necessary permissions

When you publish a message to a topic, Amazon SNS sends the message to every subscribed queue

AWS Step Functions

AWS Step Functions is used to build distributed applications as a series of steps in a visual workflow

You can quickly build and run state machines to execute the steps of your application

Managed workflow and orchestration platform

Scalable and highly available

Define your app as a state machine

Create tasks, sequential steps, parallel steps, branching paths or timers

Amazon EventBridge

Serverless event bus for building event-driven applications

Events are generated by custom applications, SaaS applications, and AWS services

An event is a signal that a system's state has changed

Route events to AWS service targets and API destinations (via HTTP endpoints)

AWS service targets include Lambda, SNS, SQS and API Gateway

API Gateway

API Gateway is a fully managed service for publishing, maintaining, monitoring, and securing APIs

An API endpoint type refers to the hostname of the API

All of the APIs created with Amazon API Gateway expose HTTPS endpoints only

The API endpoint type can be:

- Edge-optimized – for global user base
- Regional – for regional user base
- Private – within VPC or across DX connection

API Gateway - Caching

You can add caching to API calls by provisioning an Amazon API Gateway cache and specifying its size in gigabytes

Caching allows you to cache the endpoint's response

Caching can reduce number of calls to the backend and improve latency of requests to the API

API Gateway - Throttling

API Gateway sets a limit on a steady-state rate and a burst of request submissions against all APIs in your account

Limits:

- By default API Gateway limits the steady-state request rate to 10,000 requests per second

- The maximum concurrent requests is 5,000 requests across all APIs within an AWS account
- If you go over 10,000 requests per second or 5,000 concurrent requests you will receive a 429 Too Many Requests error response

Upon catching such exceptions, the client can resubmit the failed requests in a way that is rate limiting, while complying with the API Gateway throttling limits

DATABASES AND ANALYTICS

AWS Databases

Data Store	Use Case
Database on EC2	• Need full control over instance and database • Third-party database engine (not available in RDS)
Amazon RDS	• Need traditional relational database • e.g. Oracle, PostgreSQL, Microsoft SQL, MariaDB, MySQL • Data is well-formed and structured
Amazon DynamoDB	• NoSQL database • In-memory performance • High I/O needs • Dynamic scaling
Amazon RedShift	• Data warehouse for large volumes of aggregated data
Amazon ElastiCache	• Fast temporary storage for small amounts of data • In-memory database
Amazon EMR	• Analytics workloads using the Hadoop framework

Amazon RDS

RDS uses EC2 instances, so you must choose an instance family/type

Relational databases are known as Structured Query Language (SQL) databases

RDS is an Online Transaction Processing (OLTP) type of database

Easy to setup, highly available, fault tolerant, and scalable

Common use cases include online stores and banking systems

You can encrypt your Amazon RDS instances and snapshots at rest by enabling the encryption option for your Amazon RDS DB instance (during creation)

Encryption uses AWS Key Management Service (KMS)

Amazon RDS

Amazon RDS supports the following database engines:

- SQL Server
- Oracle
- MySQL Server
- PostgreSQL
- Aurora
- MariaDB

Scales up by increasing instance size (compute and storage)

Read replicas option for read heavy workloads (scales out for reads/queries only)

Disaster recovery with Multi-AZ option

Amazon RDS Multi-AZ and Read Replicas

Multi-AZ Deployments	Read Replicas
Synchronous replication – highly durable	Asynchronous replication – highly scalable
Only database engine on primary instance is active	All read replicas are accessible and can be used for read scaling
Automated backups are taken from standby	No backups configured by default
Always span two Availability Zones within a single Region	Can be within an Availability Zone, Cross-AZ, or Cross-Region

© 2026 Digital Cloud Training

Database engine version upgrades happen on primary	Database engine version upgrade is independent from source instance
Automatic failover to standby when a problem is detected	Can be manually promoted to a standalone database instance

Amazon RDS Manual Backups (Snapshot)

Backs up the entire DB instance, not just individual databases

For single-AZ DB instances there is a brief suspension of I/O

For Multi-AZ SQL Server, I/O activity is briefly suspended on primary

For Multi-AZ MariaDB, MySQL, Oracle and PostgreSQL the snapshot is taken from the standby

Snapshots do not expire (no retention period)

Amazon RDS Maintenance Windows

Operating system and DB patching can require taking the database offline

These tasks take place during a maintenance window

By default a weekly maintenance window is configured

You can choose your own maintenance window

Amazon RDS Security

Encryption at rest can be enabled – includes DB storage, backups, read replicas and snapshots

You can only enable encryption for an Amazon RDS DB instance when you create it, not after the DB instance is created

DB instances that are encrypted can't be modified to disable encryption

Uses AES 256 encryption and encryption is transparent with minimal performance impact

RDS for Oracle and SQL Server is also supported using Transparent Data Encryption (TDE) (may have performance impact)

AWS KMS is used for managing encryption keys

Amazon RDS Security

You can't have:

- An encrypted read replica of an unencrypted DB instance
- An unencrypted read replica of an encrypted DB instance

Read replicas of encrypted primary instances are encrypted

The same KMS key is used if in the same Region as the primary

If the read replica is in a different Region, a different KMS key is used

You can't restore an unencrypted backup or snapshot to an encrypted DB instance

Amazon Aurora

Amazon Aurora is an AWS database offering in the RDS family

Amazon Aurora is a MySQL and PostgreSQL-compatible relational database built for the cloud

Amazon Aurora is up to five times faster than standard MySQL databases and three times faster than standard PostgreSQL databases

Amazon Aurora features a distributed, fault-tolerant, self-healing storage system that auto-scales up to 128TB per database instance

Amazon Aurora Key Features

Aurora Feature	Benefit
High performance and scalability	Offers high performance, self-healing storage that scales up to 128TB, point-in-time recovery and continuous backup to S3
DB compatibility	Compatible with existing MySQL and PostgreSQL open source databases
Aurora Replicas	In-region read scaling and failover target – up to 15 (can use Auto Scaling)

MySQL Read Replicas	Cross-region cluster with read scaling and failover target – up to 5 (each can have up to 15 Aurora Replicas)
Global Database	Cross-region cluster with read scaling (fast replication / low latency reads). Can remove secondary and promote
Multi-Master	Scales out writes within a region
Serverless	On-demand, autoscaling configuration for Amazon Aurora - does not support read replicas or public IPs (can only access through VPC or Direct Connect - not VPN)

Amazon Aurora Replicas

Feature	Aurora Replica	MySQL Replica
Number of replicas	Up to 15	Up to 5
Replication type	Asynchronous (milliseconds)	Asynchronous (seconds)
Performance impact on primary	Low	High
Replica location	In-region	Cross-region
Act as failover target	Yes (no data loss)	Yes (potentially minutes of data loss)
Automated failover	Yes	No
Support for user-defined replication delay	No	Yes

| Support for different data or schema vs. primary | No | Yes |

Aurora Serverless Use Cases

Infrequently used applications

New applications

Variable workloads

Unpredictable workloads

Development and test databases

Multi-tenant applications

When NOT to use Amazon RDS (anti-patterns)

Anytime you need a DB type other than:
- MySQL
- MariaDB
- SQL Server
- Oracle
- PostgreSQL

You need root access to the OS (e.g. install software such as management tools)

When NOT to use Amazon RDS (anti-patterns)

Requirement	More Suitable Service
Lots of large binary objects (BLOBs)	S3
Automated Scalability	DynamoDB
Name/Value Data Structure	DynamoDB
Data is not well structured or unpredictable	DynamoDB

Other database platforms like IBM DB2 or SAP HANA	EC2
Complete control over the database	EC2

Database on Amazon EC2

You can run any database you like with full control and ultimate flexibility

You must manage everything like backups, redundancy, patching and scaling

Amazon ElastiCache

Fully managed implementations Redis and Memcached

ElastiCache is a key/value store

In-memory database offering high performance and low latency

Can be put in front of databases such as RDS and DynamoDB

ElastiCache nodes run on Amazon EC2 instances, so you must choose an instance family/type

Amazon ElastiCache

Feature	Memcached	Redis (cluster mode disabled)	Redis (cluster mode enabled)
Data persistence	No	Yes	Yes
Data types	Simple	Complex	Complex
Data partitioning	Yes	No	Yes
Encryption	No	Yes	Yes
High availability (replication)	No	Yes	Yes

Multi-AZ	Yes, place nodes in multiple AZs. No failover or replication	Yes, with auto-failover. Uses read replicas (0-5 per shard)	Yes, with auto-failover. Uses read replicas (0-5 per shard)
Scaling	Up (node type); out (add nodes)	Up (node type); out (add replica)	Up (node type); out (add shards)
Multithreaded	Yes	No	No
Backup and restore	No (and no snapshots)	Yes, automatic and manual snapshots	Yes, automatic and manual snapshots

Amazon ElastiCache Use Cases

Data that is relatively static and frequently accessed

Applications that are tolerant of stale data

Data is slow and expensive to get compared to cache retrieval

Require push-button scalability for memory, writes and reads

Often used for storing session state

Amazon DynamoDB

Fully managed NoSQL database service

Key/value store and document store

Fully serverless service

Push button scaling

Can achieve ACID compliance with DynamoDB Transactions

Data is synchronously replicated across 3 facilities (AZs) in a region

DynamoDB is schema-less

DynamoDB can be used for storing session state

Amazon DynamoDB

Provides two read models.

- Eventually consistent reads (Default)
- Strongly consistent reads

There are two pricing models for DynamoDB:

- On-demand capacity mode: DynamoDB charges you for the data reads and writes your application performs on your tables
- Provisioned capacity mode: you specify the number of reads and writes per second that you expect your application to require (can use Auto Scaling)

DynamoDB Time to Live (TTL)

TTL lets you define when items in a table expire so that they can be automatically deleted from the database

With TTL enabled on a table, you can set a timestamp for deletion on a per-item basis

No extra cost and does not use WCU / RCU

Helps reduce storage and manage the table size over time

Amazon DynamoDB

DynamoDB Feature	Benefit
Serverless	Fully managed, fault tolerant, service
Highly available	99.99% availability SLA – 99.999% for Global Tables!
NoSQL type of database with Name / Value structure	Flexible schema, good for when data is not well structured or unpredictable
Horizontal scaling	Seamless scalability to any scale with push button scaling or Auto Scaling

DynamoDB Streams	Captures a time-ordered sequence of item-level modifications in a DynamoDB table and durably stores the information for up to 24 hours. Often used with Lambda and the Kinesis Client Library (KCL)
DynamoDB Accelerator (DAX)	Fully managed in-memory cache for DynamoDB that increases performance (microsecond latency)
Transaction options	Strongly consistent or eventually consistent reads, support for ACID transactions
Backup	Point-in-time recovery down to the second in last 35 days; On-demand backup and restore
Global Tables	Fully managed multi-region, multi-master solution

DynamoDB Streams

Captures a time-ordered sequence of item-level modifications in any DynamoDB table and stores this information in a log for up to 24 hours

Can configure the information that is written to the stream:

- **KEYS_ONLY** — Only the key attributes of the modified item
- **NEW_IMAGE** — The entire item, as it appears after it was modified
- **OLD_IMAGE** — The entire item, as it appeared before it was modified
- **NEW_AND_OLD_IMAGES** — Both the new and the old images of the item

DynamoDB Accelerator (DAX)

DAX is a fully managed, highly available, in-memory cache for DynamoDB

Improves performance from milliseconds to microseconds

Can be a read-through cache and a write-through cache

Used to improve READ and WRITE performance

DAX is updated only if DynamoDB is successfully updated first

You do not need to modify application logic, since DAX is compatible with existing DynamoDB API calls

DAX vs ElastiCache

DAX is optimized for DynamoDB

With ElastiCache you have more management overhead (e.g. invalidation)

With ElastiCache you need to modify application code to point to cache

ElastiCache supports more datastores

RedShift Use Cases

Perform complex queries on massive collections of structured and semi-structured data and get fast performance

Frequently accessed data that needs a consistent, highly structured format

Use Spectrum for direct access of S3 objects in a data lake

Managed data warehouse solution with:

- Automated provisioning, configuration and patching
- Data durability with continuous backup to S3
- Scales with simple API calls
- Exabyte scale query capability

Amazon EMR

Managed cluster platform that simplifies running big data frameworks including Apache Hadoop and Apache Spark

Used for processing data for analytics and business intelligence

Can also be used for transforming and moving large amounts of data

Performs extract, transform, and load (ETL) functions

Amazon Kinesis Data Streams

Kinesis Data Streams enables real-time processing of streaming big data

Used for rapidly moving data off data producers and then continuously processing the data

Producers send data to Kinesis, data is stored in Shards for 24 hours (by default, up to 7 days)

Consumers then take the data and process it - data can then be saved into another AWS service

Kinesis Data Streams stores data for later processing by applications (key difference with Firehose which delivers data directly to AWS services)

Real time (~200ms)

Kinesis Client Library (KCL)

The Kinesis Client Library (KCL) helps you consume and process data from a Kinesis data stream

Each shard is processed by exactly one KCL worker and has exactly one corresponding record processor

One worker can process any number of shards, so it's fine if the number of shards exceeds the number of instances

Kinesis Data Firehose

Captures, transforms, and loads streaming data

Producers send data to Firehose

There are no Shards, completely automated (scalability is elastic)

Firehose data is sent to another AWS service for storing, data can be optionally processed/transformed using AWS Lambda

Enables near real-time analytics with existing business intelligence tools and dashboards

Near real-time delivery (~60 seconds latency)

Kinesis Data Firehose

Kinesis Data Firehose destinations:
- RedShift (via an intermediate S3 bucket)
- Elasticsearch
- Amazon S3
- Splunk
- Datadog
- MongoDB

- New Relic
- HTTP Endpoint

Kinesis Data Analytics

Provides real-time SQL processing for streaming data

Provides analytics for data coming in from Kinesis Data Streams and Kinesis Data Firehose

Destinations can be Kinesis Data Streams, Kinesis Data Firehose, or AWS Lambda

Quickly author and run powerful SQL code against streaming sources

Can ingest data from Kinesis Streams and Kinesis Firehose

Amazon Athena

Athena queries data in S3 using SQL

Can be connected to other data sources with Lambda

Data can be in CSV, TSV, JSON, Parquet and ORC formats

Uses a managed Data Catalog (AWS Glue) to store information and schemas about the databases and tables

Optimizing Athena for Performance

Partition your data

Bucket your data – bucket the data within a single partition

Use Compression – AWS recommend using either Apache Parquet or Apache ORC

Optimize file sizes

Optimize columnar data store generation – Apache Parquet and Apache ORC are popular columnar data stores

Optimize ORDER BY and Optimize GROUP BY

Use approximate functions

Only include the columns that you need

AWS Glue

Fully managed extract, transform and load (ETL) service

Used for preparing data for analytics

AWS Glue runs the ETL jobs on a fully managed, scale-out Apache Spark environment

AWS Glue discovers data and stores the associated metadata (e.g. table definition and schema) in the AWS Glue Data Catalog

Works with data lakes (e.g. data on S3), data warehouses (including RedShift), and data stores (including RDS or EC2 databases)

AWS Glue

You can use a crawler to populate the AWS Glue Data Catalog with tables

A crawler can crawl multiple data stores in a single run

Upon completion, the crawler creates or updates one or more tables in your Data Catalog.

ETL jobs that you define in AWS Glue use the Data Catalog tables as sources and targets

DEPLOYMENT AND MANAGEMENT

AWS CloudFormation

CloudFormation deploys infrastructure using code (JSON or YAML)

Infrastructure is provisioned consistently, with fewer mistakes (less human error)

Less time and effort than configuring resources manually

You can use version control and peer review for your CloudFormation templates

Free to use (you're only charged for the resources provisioned)

Can be used to manage updates and dependencies

Can be used to rollback and delete the entire stack as well

AWS CloudFormation

Component	Description
Templates	The JSON or YAML text file that contains the instructions for building out the AWS environment
Stacks	The entire environment described by the template and created, updated, and deleted as a single unit
StackSets	AWS CloudFormation StackSets extends the functionality of stacks by enabling you to create, update, or delete stacks across multiple accounts and regions with a single operation
Change Sets	A summary of proposed changes to your stack that will allow you to see how those changes might impact your existing resources before implementing them

AWS Elastic Beanstalk

AWS Elastic Beanstalk can be used to quickly deploy and manage applications in the AWS Cloud

Considered a Platform as a Service (PaaS) solution

Developers upload applications and Elastic Beanstalk handles the deployment details of capacity provisioning, load balancing, auto-scaling, and application health monitoring

Supports Java, .NET, PHP, Node.js, Python, Ruby, Go, and Docker web applications

There are several layers

Applications:

- Contain environments, environment configurations, and application versions
- You can have multiple application versions held within an application

Application version

- A specific reference to a section of deployable code
- The application version will point typically to an Amazon S3 bucket containing the code

Environments:

- An application version that has been deployed on AWS resources
- The resources are configured and provisioned by AWS Elastic Beanstalk
- The environment is comprised of all the resources created by Elastic Beanstalk and not just an EC2 instance with your uploaded code

Web Servers and Workers

Web servers are standard applications that listen for and then process HTTP requests, typically over port 80

Workers are specialized applications that have a background processing task that listens for messages on an Amazon SQS queue

Workers should be used for long-running tasks

AWS SSM Parameter Store

Parameter Store provides secure, hierarchical storage for configuration data and secrets

Highly scalable, available, and durable

Store data such as passwords, database strings, and license codes as parameter values

Store values as plaintext (unencrypted data) or ciphertext (encrypted data)

Reference values by using the unique name that you specified when you created the parameter

No native rotation of keys (difference with AWS Secrets Manager which does it automatically)

AWS Config

Evaluate your AWS resource configurations for desired settings

Get a snapshot of the current configurations of resources that are associated with your AWS account

Retrieve configurations of resources that exist in your account

Retrieve historical configurations of one or more resources

Receive a notification whenever a resource is created, modified, or deleted

View relationships between resources

AWS Secrets Manager

Stores and rotate secrets safely without the need for code deployments

Secrets Manager offers automatic rotation of credentials (built-in) for:

- Amazon RDS (MySQL, PostgreSQL, and Amazon Aurora)
- Amazon Redshift
- Amazon DocumentDB

For other services you can write your own AWS Lambda function for automatic rotation

AWS Secrets Manager vs SSM Parameter Store

	Secrets Manager	SSM Parameter Store

Automatic Key Rotation	Yes, built-in for some services, use Lambda for others	No native key rotation; can use custom Lambda
Key/Value Type	String or Binary (encrypted)	String, StringList, SecureString (encrypted)
Hierarchical Keys	No	Yes
Price	Charges apply per secret	Free for standard, charges for advanced

AWS OpsWorks

AWS OpsWorks is a configuration management service that provides managed instances of Chef and Puppet

Updates include patching, updating, backup, configuration and compliance management

AWS RAM

Shares resources:

- Across AWS accounts
- Within AWS Organizations or OUs
- IAM roles and IAM users

Resource shares are created with:

- The AWS RAM Console
- AWS RAM APIs
- AWS CLI
- AWS SDKs

RAM can be used to share:

- AWS App Mesh
- Amazon Aurora
- AWS Certificate Manager Private Certificate Authority
- AWS CodeBuild

- Amazon EC2
- EC2 Image Builder
- AWS Glue
- AWS License Manager
- AWS Network Firewall
- AWS Outposts
- Amazon S3 on Outposts
- AWS Resource Groups
- Amazon Route 53
- AWS Systems Manager Incident Manager
- Amazon VPC

MONITORING, LOGGING, AND AUDITING

Amazon CloudWatch

CloudWatch is used for performance monitoring, alarms, log collection and automated actions

Use cases / benefits include:

- Collect performance metrics from AWS and on-premises systems
- Automate responses to operational changes
- Improve operational performance and resource optimization
- Derive actionable insights from logs
- Get operational visibility and insight

CloudWatch Core Features:

- **CloudWatch Metrics** – services send time-ordered data points to CloudWatch
- **CloudWatch Alarms** – monitor metrics and initiate actions
- **CloudWatch Logs** – centralized collection of system and application logs
- **CloudWatch Events** – stream of system events describing changes to AWS resources and can trigger actions

Amazon CloudWatch Metrics

Metrics are sent to CloudWatch for many AWS services

EC2 metrics are sent every 5 minutes by default (free)

Detailed EC2 monitoring sends every 1 minute (chargeable)

Unified CloudWatch Agent sends system-level metrics for EC2 and on-premises servers

System-level metrics include memory and disk usage

Can publish custom metrics using CLI or API

Custom metrics are one of the following resolutions:

- **Standard resolution** – data having a one-minute granularity
- **High resolution** – data at a granularity of one second

AWS metrics are standard resolution by default

Amazon CloudWatch Alarms

Two types of alarms

Metric alarm – performs one or more actions based on a single metric

Composite alarm – uses a rule expression and takes into account multiple alarms

Metric alarm states:

- OK – Metric is within a threshold
- ALARM – Metric is outside a threshold
- INSUFFICIENT_DATA – not enough data

Amazon CloudWatch Logs

Gather application and system logs in CloudWatch

Define expiration policies and KMS encryption

Send to:

- Amazon S3 (export)
- Kinesis Data Streams
- Kinesis Data Firehose

The Unified CloudWatch Agent

The unified CloudWatch agent enables you to do the following:

- Collect internal system-level metrics from Amazon EC2 instances across operating systems
- Collect system-level metrics from on-premises servers
- Retrieve custom metrics from your applications or services using the StatsD and collectd protocols
- Collect logs from Amazon EC2 instances and on-premises servers (Windows / Linux)

Agent must be installed on the server

Can be installed on:

- Amazon EC2 instances
- On-premises servers

- Linux, Windows Server, or macOS

AWS CloudTrail

CloudTrail logs API activity for auditing

By default, management events are logged and retained for 90 days

A CloudTrail Trail logs any events to S3 for indefinite retention

Trail can be within Region or all Regions

CloudWatch Events can triggered based on API calls in CloudTrail

Events can be streamed to CloudWatch Logs

CloudTrail – Types of Events

Management events provide information about management operations that are performed on resources in your AWS account

Data events provide information about the resource operations performed on or in a resource

Insights events identify and respond to unusual activity associated with write API calls by continuously analyzing CloudTrail management events

SECURITY IN THE CLOUD

AWS Managed Microsoft AD

Fully managed AWS service

Best choice if you have more than 5000 users and/or need a trust relationship set up

Can perform schema extensions

Can setup trust relationships with on-premises Active Directories:

- On-premise users and groups can access resources in either domain using SSO
- Requires a VPN or Direct Connect connection

Can be used as a standalone AD in the AWS cloud

AD Connector

Redirects directory requests to your on-premises Active Directory

Best choice when you want to use an existing Active Directory with AWS services

AD Connector comes in two sizes:

- Small – designed for organizations up to 500 users
- Large – designed for organizations up to 5000 users

Requires a VPN or Direct Connect connection

Join EC2 instances to your on-premises AD through AD Connector

Login to the AWS Management Console using your on-premises AD DCs for authentication

Simple AD

Inexpensive Active Directory-compatible service with common directory features

Standalone, fully managed, directory on the AWS cloud

Simple AD is generally the least expensive option

Best choice for less than 5000 users and don't need advanced AD features

Features include:

- Manage user accounts / groups
- Apply group policies
- Kerberos-based SSO
- Supports joining Linux or Windows based EC2 instances

Identity Providers and Federation

With an identity provider (IdP), you can manage user identities outside of AWS and give these identities permissions to use AWS resources in your account.

For example:

- Your organization already has its own identity system, such as a corporate user directory
- You're creating a mobile app or web application that requires access to AWS resources

With an IAM identity provider, there's no need to create custom sign-in code or manage your own user identities. The IdP provides that for you

External users sign in through a well-known IdP, such as Login with Amazon, Facebook, or Google.

IAM supports IdPs that are compatible with OpenID Connect (OIDC) or SAML 2.0 (Security Assertion Markup Language 2.0)

AWS Single Sign-On

Centrally manage access to multiple AWS accounts and business applications

Easily manage SSO access and user permissions to all your accounts in AWS Organizations centrally

AWS SSO also includes built-in integrations to many business applications, such as Salesforce, Box, and Office 365

Create and manage user identities in AWS SSO's identity store

Or connect to existing identity store such as Microsoft AD or Azure

Amazon Cognito

Add user sign-up, sign-in, and access control to your web and mobile apps

A User Pool is a directory for managing sign-in and sign-up

Users can be stored in a User Pool or can sign in using social IdPs

Supports SAML and OIDC IdPs

Cognito acts as an Identity Broker between the IdP and AWS

Identity pools are used to obtain temporary, limited-privilege credentials for AWS services (using STS)

An IAM role is assumed, providing access to the AWS services

AWS Key Management Service (KMS)

Fully-managed service that enables you to create and manage cryptographic keys

Can control key usage across AWS services and in applications

AWS KMS allows you to centrally manage and securely store your keys

Supports symmetric and asymmetric encryption

Customer Master Keys (CMKs)

Customer master keys are the primary resources in AWS KMS

The CMK also contains the key material used to encrypt and decrypt data

CMKs are created in AWS KMS

Symmetric CMKs and the private keys of asymmetric CMKs never leave AWS KMS unencrypted

By default, AWS KMS creates the key material for a CMK

Can also import your own key material

A CMK can encrypt data up to 4KB in size

A CMK can generate, encrypt and decrypt Data Encryption Keys

Data Encryption Keys can be used for encrypting large amounts of data

AWS Managed CMKs

Created, managed, and used on your behalf by an AWS service that is integrated with AWS KMS

You cannot manage these CMKs, rotate them, or change their key policies

You also cannot use AWS managed CMKs in cryptographic operations directly; the service that creates them uses them on your behalf

Data Encryption Keys

Data keys are encryption keys that you can use to encrypt data, including large amounts of data and other data encryption keys

You can use AWS KMS customer master keys (CMKs) to generate, encrypt, and decrypt data keys

AWS KMS does not store, manage, or track your data keys, or perform cryptographic operations with data keys

You must use and manage data keys outside of AWS KMS

Customer Master Keys (CMKs)

Type of CMK	Can view	Can manage	Used only for my AWS account	Automatic rotation
Customer managed CMK	Yes	Yes	Yes	Optional. Every 365 days
AWS managed CMK	Yes	No	Yes	Required. Every 1095 days
AWS owned CMK	No	No	No	Varies

AWS CloudHSM

AWS CloudHSM is a cloud-based hardware security module (HSM)

Generate and use your own encryption keys on the AWS Cloud

CloudHSM runs in your Amazon VPC

Uses FIPS 140-2 level 3 validated HSMs

Managed service and automatically scales

Retain control of your encryption keys - you control access (and AWS has no visibility of your encryption keys)

AWS CloudHSM Use Cases

Offload SSL/TLS processing from web servers

Protect private keys for an issuing certificate authority (CA)

Store the master key for Oracle DB Transparent Data Encryption

Custom key store for AWS KMS – retain control of the HSM that protects the master keys

AWS CloudHSM vs KMS

	CloudHSM	**AWS KMS**
Tenancy	Single-tenant HSM	Multi-tenant AWS service
Availability	Customer-managed durability and available	Highly available and durable key storage and management
Root of Trust	Customer managed root of trust	AWS managed root of trust
FIPS 140-2	Level 3	Level 2 / Level 3
3rd Party Support	Broad 3rd Party Support	Broad AWS service support

AWS Certificate Manager (ACM)

Create, store and renew SSL/TLS X.509 certificates

Single domains, multiple domain names and wildcards

Integrates with several AWS services including:
- Elastic Load Balancing
- Amazon CloudFront
- AWS Elastic Beanstalk
- AWS Nitro Enclaves
- AWS CloudFormation

Public certificates are signed by the AWS public Certificate Authority

You can also create a Private CA with ACM

Can then issue private certificates

You can also import certificates from third-party issuers

AWS WAF

AWS WAF is a web application firewall

WAF lets you create rules to filter web traffic based on conditions that include IP addresses, HTTP headers and body, or custom URIs

WAF makes it easy to create rules that block common web exploits like SQL injection and cross site scripting

Web ACLs – You use a web access control list (ACL) to protect a set of AWS resources

Rules – Each rule contains a statement that defines the inspection criteria, and an action to take if a web request meets the criteria

Rule groups – You can use rules individually or in reusable rule groups

IP Sets - An IP set provides a collection of IP addresses and IP address ranges that you want to use together in a rule statement

Regex pattern set - A regex pattern set provides a collection of regular expressions that you want to use together in a rule statement

A rule action tells AWS WAF what to do with a web request when it matches the criteria defined in the rule:

Count – AWS WAF counts the request but doesn't determine whether to allow it or block it. With this action, AWS WAF continues processing the remaining rules in the web ACL

Allow – AWS WAF allows the request to be forwarded to the AWS resource for processing and response

Block – AWS WAF blocks the request and the AWS resource responds with an HTTP 403 (Forbidden) status code

Match statements compare the web request or its origin against conditions that you provide

Match Statement	Description
Geographic match	Inspects the request's country of origin
IP set match	Inspects the request against a set of IP addresses and address ranges
Regex pattern set	Compares regex patterns against a specified request component
Size constraint	Checks size constraints against a specified request component
SQLi attack	Inspects for malicious SQL code in a specified request component
String match	Compares a string to a specified request component
XSS scripting attack	Inspects for cross-site scripting attacks in a specified request component

AWS Shield

AWS Shield is a managed Distributed Denial of Service (DDoS) protection service

Safeguards web application running on AWS with always-on detection and automatic inline mitigations

Helps to minimize application downtime and latency

Two tiers –

Standard – no cost

Advanced - $3k USD per month and 1 year commitment

Integrated with Amazon CloudFront (standard included by default)

MIGRATION AND TRANSFER SERVICES

AWS Server Migration Service (SMS)

Agentless service for migrating on-premises and cloud-based VMs to AWS

Source platforms can be VMware, Hyper-V or Azure

AWS Server Migration Service Connector is installed on the source platform

Server volumes are replicated (encrypted with TLS) and saved as AMIs which can then be launched as EC2 instances

Can use application groupings and SMS will launch servers in a CloudFormation stack

You can replicate your on-premises servers to AWS for up to 90 days (per server)

Provides automated, live incremental server replication and AWS Console support

AWS Database Migration Service (DMS)

Use to migrate databases from on-premises, Amazon EC2 or Amazon RDS

Supports homogenous (e.g. Oracle to Oracle) as well as heterogenous (e.g. Oracle to Amazon Aurora)

Data is continuously replicated while the application is live, minimizing downtime

Pay based on compute resources used during the migration and log storage

Fully managed migration process

Use with the Schema Conversion tool for converting schemas

AWS DMS Use Cases

Cloud to Cloud – EC2 to RDS, RDS to RDS, RDS to Aurora

On-Premises to Cloud

Homogeneous migrations – Oracle to Oracle, MySQL to RDS MySQL, Microsoft SQL to RDS for SQL Server

Heterogeneous migrations – Oracle to Aurora, Oracle to PostgreSQL, Microsoft SQL to RDS MySQL (must convert schema first wit the Shema Conversion Tool (SCT))

Development and Test – use the cloud for dev/test workloads

Database consolidation – consolidate multiple source DBs to a single target DB

Continuous Data Replication – use for DR, dev/test, single source multi-target or multi-source single target

AWS DataSync

DataSync software agent connects to on-premises NAS storage systems

The NAS can use NFS or SMB protocols

Synchronizes data into AWS using a Scheduled, automated data transfer with TLS encryption

Destination can be Amazon S3, Amazon EFS or Amazon FSx for Windows File Server

Can improve performance for data transfers up to 10x faster than traditional tooling

Permissions and metadata are preserved

Pay per-GB transferred

AWS Snowball Family

AWS Snowball and Snowmobile are used for migrating large volumes of data to AWS

Snowball Edge Compute Optimized

- Provides block and object storage and optional GPU
- Use for data collection, machine learning and processing, and storage in environments with intermittent connectivity (edge use cases)

Snowball Edge Storage Optimized

- Provides block storage and Amazon S3-compatible object storage
- Use for local storage and large-scale data transfer

Snowcone

- Small device used for edge computing, storage and data transfer
- Can transfer data offline or online with AWS DataSync agent

Uses a secure storage device for physical transportation

Snowball Client is software that is installed on a local computer and is used to identify, compress, encrypt, and transfer data

Uses 256-bit encryption (managed with the AWS KMS) and tamper-resistant enclosures with TPM

Snowball (80TB) (50TB) "petabyte scale"

Snowball Edge (100TB) "petabyte scale"

Snowmobile – "exabyte scale" with up to 100PB per Snowmobile

Ways to optimize the performance of Snowball transfers:

1. Use the latest Mac or Linux Snowball client
2. Batch small files together
3. Perform multiple copy operations at one time
4. Copy from multiple workstations
5. Transfer directories, not files

AWS Snowball Use Cases

Cloud data migration – migrate data to the cloud

Content distribution – send data to clients or customers

Tactical Edge Computing – collect data and compute

Machine learning – run ML directly on the device

Manufacturing – data collection and analysis in the factory

Remote locations with simple data – pre-processing, tagging, compression etc.

CONCLUSION

We trust that these training resources have provided you with a clear and thorough understanding of the key concepts needed to pass the AWS Certified Solutions Architect Associate exam on your first attempt.

The exam covers a wide range of technologies, so it's essential that you're equipped with the knowledge to answer whatever question comes up in your certification exam. We recommend reviewing the exam cram thoroughly until you feel confident in all areas.

Assess your Exam Readiness with Practice Exams

The Digital Cloud Training practice questions are the closest to the actual exam and the only exam-difficulty questions on the market. If you can pass these mock exams, you're well set to ace the real thing.

To learn more, visit https://digitalcloud.training/aws-certified-solutions-architect-associate.

Reach Out and Connect

We're committed to providing you with a 5-star learning experience. If something isn't meeting your expectations, don't hesitate to email us at support@digitalcloud.training. We're here to address any questions or concerns you may have and ensure you get the most value from these training resources.

The AWS platform is evolving quickly, and the exam tracks these changes, typically with a 6-month delay. To stay up to date, we rely on feedback from students like you. If you encounter topics on your exam that weren't covered in our training materials, we'd greatly appreciate your input.

Please share your feedback using this form: https://digitalcloud.training/student-feedback. Your feedback is invaluable in helping us continuously improve our AWS training resources. Thank you for helping us make these materials even better!

How to Access your Video Course

As a special bonus, we are now offering **FREE access to the video course** on the Digital Cloud Training website with 24 hours of high-quality lessons.

To gain FREE access to the course, simply send email us at csaaexamcram@digitalcloud.training with a **proof of purchase of this book** (from Amazon) attached and "**CSAAEXAMCRAM**" in the subject line. You will then be granted FREE access to our video course within 48 hours. Should you encounter ANY problems in the process, please reach out via support@digitalcloud.training. We're here to support you on your cloud journey.

Leave us a Review

Your reviews help us improve our courses and help your fellow AWS students make the right choices. We celebrate every honest review and truly appreciate it. You can leave a review at any time by visiting amazon.com/ryp or your local amazon store (e.g. amazon.co.uk/ryp).

Best wishes for your AWS certification journey!

LIVE BOOTCAMPS AND ON-DEMAND TRAINING

Digital Cloud Training offers a wide range of training options to help students prepare for AWS certification exams and build job-ready cloud skills. Below is an overview of the available learning options.

Cloud Mastery Bootcamp (virtual classroom)

The Cloud Mastery Bootcamp is Digital Cloud Training's flagship program, designed to help you build the in-demand cloud skills needed to excel in today's competitive cloud industry. This isn't just another training - it's a structured path toward securing a high-paying, future-proof career in cloud computing - guaranteed!

This hands-on program prepares learners to highly paid cloud roles, like Cloud Engineer, DevOps Engineer, or Solutions Architect. Whether you're just beginning your cloud journey or looking to deepen your expertise, the Cloud Mastery Bootcamp provides everything you need to succeed:

- **Customized Learning Path**: Upon enrollment, we'll create a personalized learning path tailored to your skills and career goals, helping you get the most from this 12-month program.
- **Gain Hands-On Experience:** Build practical, job-ready skills by working on real-world projects with direct access to expert instructors during live training sessions (via zoom).
- **Earn Recognized Certifications**: Prepare for in-demand cloud certifications like AWS Cloud Practitioner, AWS AI Practitioner, AWS Solutions Architect, AWS Developer, AWS CloudOps Engineer or Terraform Associate.
- **Comprehensive Support**: Benefit from personalized mentoring, career coaching, and ongoing guidance from our dedicated support team to help you stay motivated and on track.
- **Launch Your Cloud Career**: Leverage your new skills, experience, and certifications to secure a high-paying job in cloud computing.

With no specific prerequisites, this program is accessible to anyone ready to begin or advance their career in the cloud.

Secure your next-level cloud job with the Cloud Mastery Bootcamp: https://digitalcloud.training/cloud-mastery-bootcamp/

On-demand / self-paced AWS Training

Prepare for your next AWS certification with flexible, cost-effective, self-paced training. Our on-demand courses include video lessons, practice exams, and downloadable training notes for offline study.

A single subscription gives you unlimited access to our entire training library, along with early access to new content and updates. Whether you select a monthly plan for full flexibility or a 12-month option to maximize savings, you'll have everything you need to build your cloud expertise at your own pace.

Explore our full library of AWS training courses:
https://digitalcloud.training/plans/

ABOUT THE AUTHOR

Neal Davis is the founder of Digital Cloud Training, an AWS Cloud Solutions Architect and a highly successful IT instructor. With over two decades of experience in the cloud computing industry, Neal is a recognized expert in solutions architecture.

In 2018, Neal launched Digital Cloud Training with the mission to bring the highest quality AWS learning resources to the market. His passion for teaching technology is matched by his commitment to helping learners achieve their cloud career goals.

Digital Cloud Training offers a range of top-quality training resources to help students build job-ready cloud skills – including live bootcamps and on-demand training courses.

By choosing Digital Cloud Training, you'll gain the skills, certifications, and real-world experience that will help you excel in the cloud industry and advance your career.

Join the growing AWS Community of more than 1,000,000 happy learners who have enrolled in Digital Cloud Training courses.

To learn more, visit: http://digitalcloud.training/

Connect with us on Social Media

Stay updated and engage with us on your favorite platforms.

All links available on https://digitalcloud.training/about-neal-davis-and-digital-cloud-training/

 digitalcloud.training

 youtube.com/c/digitalcloudtraining

 facebook.com/digitalcloudtraining

Twitter / X @digitalcloudt

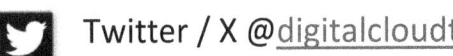 linkedin.com/company/digitalcloudtraining

Instagram @digitalcloudtraining

www.ingramcontent.com/pod-product-compliance
Lightning Source LLC
Chambersburg PA
CBHW060422220526
45465CB00008B/2981